THINGS I DIDN'T LEARN IN SEMINARY

SHORT STORIES OF A YOUNG PASTOR IN WEST BERLIN

Dr. Tim Kauffman

Copyright © 2025 by Dr. Tim Kauffman.

ISBN: 979-8-89090-272-6 (sc)
ISBN: 979-8-89090-273-3 (e)

All rights reserved. No part of this book may be reproduced or transmitted in any form or by any means, electronic or mechanical, including photocopying, recording, or by any information storage and retrieval system, without permission in writing from the copyright owner.

The views expressed in this work are solely those of the author and do not necessarily reflect the views of the publisher, and the publisher hereby disclaims any responsibility for them.

EXPRESSO

Executive Center 777, Dunsmuir Street Vancouver, BC V71K4
1-888-721-0662 ext 101
info@expressopublishing.com

DEDICATION

This book is dedicated to Mary-Esther, my amazing wife of 57 years, and strong partner during our years in West Berlin. The menial tasks she assumed until her German became very good, and her ability to minister to everyone in her orbit was grace-filled. Her ministry in the congregation, her winsome spirit, her management of our home, all the guests, and our son, was an inspiration to me.

TABLE OF CONTENTS

PROLOGUE ix
   God's Call to Germany ix
   Delay #1 ix
   Delay #2 ix
   Delay #3 x
   The Call to New Zealand x
   The Resurrection of Our Dream xi
   Lessons Learned xi

INTRODUCTION xiii
   The Church's Calling xiv
   The Book xiv

PART I: CHRIST AS ABSOLUTE LORD OF HIS CHURCH 1

CHAPTER 1—ARRIVAL IN WEST BERLIN AND THE PEOPLE 3
   The Language Barrier and Resentment 4
   Resisting the Help of Others—Generous to a Fault 5
   Forgiveness 6
   The Separation of LGBTQ+ Prejudice 6
   The Walls of Collapsing Buildings 7
   Their Stories Need to Be Heard 8

CHAPTER 2—BIG CONCEPT, BIGGER COLLAPSE 10
   Cultural Arrogance 10
   Lesson Learned 12

CHAPTER 3—BEING "IN ONE ACCORD" 13
   Cultural Insensitivity and Repentance 13
   Lesson Learned 17

CHAPTER 4—BEING MUTUALLY TRANSPARENT 20
   Confession of Faults 20
   Leaders Need to Work Together 22
   Werner Zimmermann 22
   Lessons Learned 23

CHAPTER 5—THE STEPS TOWARD SELF-SUPPORT 25
   The Wall of Self-Preservation 25
   Self-Support Is Reachable 26
   The End of the Story 27
   Lessons Learned 27

PART II: CHRIST'S FAITHFULNESS AS LORD 29

CHAPTER 6—ministry to families 31
The Wall of Dysfunction 31
How We Got Started 32
Some Topics We Came Up With 33
Time Schedule 33
Lessons Learned 34

CHAPTER 7—MENTORING LEADERS 35
The Wall of Inaccessibility 35
Multiplication 37
Mentoring the Lay Leaders 38
Lessons Learned 39
Mentoring Future Pastors 39
What Happens During an Internship? 39
The Long-Term Impact of Mentoring 40
Lessons Learned 41

CHAPTER 8—GOD WILL WATCH OVER THAT WHICH BELONGS TO HIM 42
The Wall of Our Possessions 42
Ministering to Michael 43
The VW Bus is Gone 44
The Bus is Back! 45
Lessons Learned 48

CHAPTER 9—A TIN CAN AND GOD'S PROVISION 49
The Wall of Language 49
John David's Prayer of Faith 51
Lesson Learned 52

CHAPTER 10—LILI IS BORN AT OUR HOUSE 53
Hospitality 53
Ruth Schermuly 53
Lessons Learned 57

CHAPTER 11—GOD'S HEALING POWER 58
The Wall of Timidity 58
Friedrich Behmenburg 58
Christian Hilliges 62
Klaus Dykoff 63
Lessons Learned 65

CHAPTER 12—WONDERFULLY MULTICULTURAL ... 66
A Wall That Resists Welcoming People of Color ... 66
Gloria and Carlos Gutierrez – El Salvador ... 67
Slamet, Matilde, and Tobias Basuki – Indonesia ... 67
Gisela Abraham – India ... 68
Five Politicians in Exile – Ghana ... 68
Some Stayed Briefly in our Apartment ... 69
Lessons Learned ... 70

CHAPTER 13—VENGEANCE IS MINE SAYS THE LORD ... 71
The Wall of Unforgiveness ... 71
Father Forgive Him ... 76
Lessons Learned ... 77

PART III: THE STRUGGLE OF CHRIST'S LORDSHIP ... 79

CHAPTER 14—LORD, WE CANNOT AFFORD IT ... 81
Too Little Faith ... 81
The Prayer Meeting ... 81
Christian Hilliges ... 83
Lesson Learned ... 85

CHAPTER 15—THE GATES OF HELL CANNOT RESIST HIS VICTORY ... 86
The Walls of Opposition ... 86
A New Direction ... 86
God Provides Yet another Way ... 88
The Neighbors Won ... 90
The Incredible Progression ... 90
Some Seed Will Produce a Hundred-Fold ... 91
Lessons Learned ... 92

CHAPTER 16—FUNDRAISING IN THE UNITED STATES ... 93
Barriers of Uncertainty ... 93
The Flight to Oklahoma City ... 93
The Flight to Nampa ... 94
I Want to Give It to Help Build the Church ... 96
Lessons Learned ... 98

CHAPTER 17—THOMAS AND ESTHER JOIN US ... 99
Holding on in Faith ... 99
How It All Began ... 99
Thomas and Esther Come to Help Start a Second Church ... 100
The St. James Church ... 102
Lessons Learned ... 103

CHAPTER 18—THE RENOVATION 104
Building the City 104
Moving In 105
Udo, the Painter 107
God's Protection for Thomas 107
The Villa Itself 108
Summary of the Renovation 108
Lessons Learned 109

CHAPTER 19—EVEN WHEN THE DREAM IS GONE 110
Giving Up Too Soon 110
Where Would the Second Church Be Located? 110
What a Blessing! 113
Victory Weekend 114
Saturday Evening, May 20, at 7:00 pm 114
Sunday Morning, May 21, at 11:00 am 115
Sunday evening, May 28, at 7:00 pm 115
Lessons Learned 115

CHAPTER 20—TRANSFORMED LIVES
ARE HIS REWARD 117
When Walls Come Down, Maturity and Usefulness Follow 117
Hans-Joachim Hahn 118
Andreas Herling 119
Annegrit Elsner 120
The Principle Involved 121
Lessons Learned 122

EPILOGUE 123
The Call to Frankfurt 123
Thomas and Esther 123
The Thrust to the City in Berlin 124
The Church Planting Philosophy 124
The Current Pastoral Team in Berlin and Northern Germany 126
Conclusion 127

ICHTHYS 129
The Founding of ICHTHYS 129
Frank Rudersdorf's Testimony 130
Closing 131

PERSONAL HISTORY 133
Writing: 133

ACKNOWLEDGMENTS 135

Endnotes 137

PROLOGUE

God's Call to Germany

After graduating from college, I spent a year in Frankfurt in 1965-1966 helping the German District start a printing business, not only for our own church, but for other denominations. While there, God called me into the ministry in a foreign land, but He did not tell me where it would be.

Later, in my second year at seminary, the Lord began speaking to me about returning to Germany. I was learning to trust His nudging, but I wanted to be sure. I told Mary-Esther, "Don't fix lunch for me. I need to pray." In the bedroom, on my knees, God clarified that He wanted us to serve in Germany. I was ready to go right then.

Delay #1

My mentor, Dr. Paul Orjala, listened patiently as I excitedly told him the news. When I finished, he rejoiced with me and asked, "Don't you think you would be more effective if you finished preparing first?" I had to agree, but it was the first, and not the last, wall of frustration along the way.

Delay #2

A few months before graduation, we received a call to be the assistant pastor of a large church in Western Pennsylvania. I called Germany to let them know we were available. But, because of leadership changes, the door to Germany remained closed. More delay. Why was God delaying? Why would He call us to go and then let us wait so long? As I was reading and praying, He directed me to Habakkuk 2:2-3 in the Living Bible:

PROLOGUE

"But these things I plan won't happen right away. Slowly, steadily, surely, the time approaches when the vision will be fulfilled. If it seems slow, don't despair, for these things will surely come to pass. Just be patient! They will not be overdue a single day!"

We waited, sometimes not so patiently. Six years later, in 1972, Mary-Esther and I arrived in Miami for a convention. We were early and decided to look at the publishing house booth. As we entered the Convention Hall, it was virtually empty. Standing alone at the book table was Richard Zanner, who had been my pastor in Germany, and was now its District Superintendent. We greeted each other warmly, and I introduced Mary-Esther. Immediately, he turned to me and asked, "Tim, how would you like to go back to Germany?" It was so sudden that I stammered in the affirmative but would need to talk it over with Mary-Esther and pray about it overnight. We talked a little longer and made an appointment for breakfast.

Delay #3

As soon as we returned to our hotel room, we asked God for direction. His answer was clear. He said, "Not now, wait for one year. I did not understand it, but accepted it. The next morning at breakfast, I told Richard God's answer. He accepted it, and we parted.

The Call to New Zealand

Eight months later, I received a phone call from Headquarters asking us if we would go to New Zealand. Again, I asked for time to pray and to correspond with New Zealand, which I did.

Time was not my friend. I was in agony. I decided to intervene and sat down to write Richard Zanner and ask how things stood there. I sat down and typed, "Dear Richard," but got such a heavy feeling in my spirit that I could not write another word. I begged God for some direction. Finally, God said, "Tim, if I want you in New Zealand, would you go?" I said, "Of course, Lord." I determined, when the last letter from New Zealand arrived, to spend 24 hours in prayer and make a final decision. But I felt trapped. Was the "call" to Germany my idea? I couldn't imagine it was, but maybe I had been wrong about it. The dream for Germany was dead.

The Resurrection of Our Dream

A week later, I stopped to pick up the mail on my way to the hospital for some elective surgery. Sitting in the chair waiting to be admitted, I leafed through it. On the top was the letter from New Zealand that I was expecting. In New Zealand, everything was ready for us to arrive. My heart did not feel any lighter. But I continued through the stack, and the last envelope was a letter from Richard Zanner. The two long distance letters arrived in my mailbox the same day. Then I opened the letter from Richard Zanner: "Tim, a year has gone by. The church in West Berlin is open. Would you come?" "Okay, Lord, it is crunch-time."

There I was. What to do? What about the dear, patient people in New Zealand? My vision had died. After much anguish, my mother reminded me of God's promise in Habakkuk, *"My answer won't be overdue a single day."* She counseled, "With all that has just happened, will you not always think you missed it?" It was the resurrection of God's original vision!

Lessons Learned

We learned that God can still resurrect His promise when we continue to trust. When He performs a resurrection, there are three things we can count on:

- He raised the promise with an eternal quality to it that has the power of God behind it. It gave us an overwhelming realization of being sent.
- Because God resurrected the promise, we have no claim on what He does through us.
- Had we made this vision happen in our strength alone, we would have missed the growing, ever-unfolding Kingdom plan He had for us. When God resurrects something, it lives not only today and tomorrow, but into eternity.

PROLOGUE

We found a few excited people when we arrived in Berlin in 1974. One family of five, together with us, made two families of eight, a handful of young professionals and about ten seniors. Our first month's average attendance was 19 people. It was wonderful. The church was begun in 1961, and thirteen years later, we were the seventh pastor.

Today, 49 years later, there are three churches and a compassionate ministry to addicts and the homeless celebrating 30 years of ministry. To God be the glory. It is all His doing! When God provides a resurrection, it keeps going because He is in charge.

These were the beginning of many walls and obstacles overcome by God's grace. They formed us with lessons of His power that took us, by His Grace, to a place of complete trust in His Lordship.

INTRODUCTION

*"Christian brotherhood is not an ideal that we have to realize, but it is **a reality** created by God in Christ in which we may take part:"* - Dietrich Bonhoeffer, Life Together.

The desire to write this book began when my oncologist diagnosed me in September 2020 with a highly aggressive and incurable form of lymphoma. The doctor gave me 4-6 months to live. When I asked about chemotherapy, he added that a four-month course would give me a better quality of life during that time and might extend my life a few more months.

Shocked, but determined, I confronted the question of how I could invest this precious gift of time that God had given me. We called for the pastor to anoint me and pray for healing. The family gathered around while he prayed. After the four-month course of chemotherapy, we were all astonished when the doctor told us I was in remission. Now, in April 2022, I'm still in remission! Glory to God! What a wonderful gift.

Immediately following my diagnosis, I prayed, asking God what I should do with the time He had given me. I was to write about my eight years as a pastor in West Berlin and the lessons God taught our little congregation as we journeyed together on the road to Christ's Lordship.

Some of those lessons included loving and forgiving each other, reconciliation, living together in unity, and being fully authentic with each other, which are transforming traits for the church in any era. God opened more exciting and fruitful ministries at each point of surrender.

Dietrich Bonhoeffer wrote in his book Life Together, "Christian brotherhood is not an ideal that we have to realize, but it is a reality created by God in Christ in which we may participate."[1] We were just a tiny Christian brotherhood who accepted Christ's invitation to begin walking down the road to participate in His reality.

The Church's Calling

What does all this mean? God has called the church to be His ambassadors, but how can we be ambassadors if we are not markedly different from the host culture? God's Kingdom is the visible presence of Christ's Lordship amid the "kingdoms of this world."

"We are therefore Christ's ambassadors, as though God were making his appeal through us. We implore you on Christ's behalf: Be reconciled to God." (2 Corinthians 5:20).

In other words, God wants individuals to experience Christ's Lordship for their benefit and much more. God is interested in creating shining outposts of His Kingdom, not copycats of kingdoms to which He sends us.

As more and more individuals journey on the road to Christ's Lordship, the congregation will be increasingly like its Lord.

When the Holy Spirit is honored and given control, the gifts of Christ are plentiful, but they are only visible when there is a willingness to receive them. As the walls of pride, selfishness, self-determination, etc., come down, Christ's Lordship becomes visible through His Church and will become increasingly apparent to the society around us.

The stories in this book illustrate some of those walls that God will remove along the way. If we let Him, He will transform us more and more into His image. We discovered that as the people in West Berlin committed their lives and concerns entirely to the Lordship of Christ, God's provision and guidance bordered on the miraculous.

The Book

The stories describe how God honored, directed, and blessed the West Berlin church individually and corporately as they took the road toward Christ's Lordship. The Holy Spirit broke down the walls that hindered His complete Lordship. In Chapter One, you will hear a few stories of people the War scarred forever. Chapter Two you will read how a young American pastor in Germany built his own wall. In Chapter Three, we all watch how God transformed that wall into unity and set us all on the road to Christ's Lordship for the remaining seven years. The succeeding chapters illustrate how our unity in Christ became reality step by step, culminating in transforming a villa into a church building and the birth of a second congregation. In the Epilogue, you will read how God continued to bless the ministry through Thomas and Esther Vollenweider by multiplying the church in that great city and founding ICHTHYS. This compassionate ministry has been ministering to the homeless and addicted of Berlin for over 30 years.

Allow me to invite you to take a ride with us on our first trip to West Berlin, and the first footsteps toward lessons learned on the journey to Christ's Lordship. We will meet some remarkable people there. The ride together is going to be both an adventure and an education.

PART I

CHRIST AS ABSOLUTE LORD OF HIS CHURCH

CHAPTER 1

ARRIVAL IN WEST BERLIN AND THE PEOPLE

"I easily forget that the fellowship of Christian brethren is a gift of grace, a gift of the Kingdom of God that any day may be taken from us. The time that still separates us from utter loneliness may be brief indeed. Therefore, let him, who until now has had the privilege of living a common Christian life with other Christians, praise God's grace sincerely. Let him thank God on his knees and declare: It is grace, nothing but grace, that we may live in community with Christian brethren."— Dietrich Bonhoeffer, Life Together.

It is easy to forget that the trip to West Berlin was arduous. After leaving the West German checkpoint, we had to go through an East German checkpoint at the West German border. The East German controls were deliberately slow. We could wait for over two hours to receive the precious "transit visa." During that time, they asked us questions and suspiciously compared our faces to the pictures on our passports. Then they examined the car's cabin, rummaged through the trunk, and inspected the undercarriage with mirrors and dogs. After receiving the "transit visa," we then had a 90-minute drive through East Germany along a prescribed four-lane highway[2] to West Berlin. There were strict speed and lane use rules with severe penalties for violation. If we accidentally took a wrong exit ramp, the police would stop us and either fine or put us in jail. When we finally reached the West Berlin border, the East transit controls started all over again to release us out of the East German lockup. It is hard for anyone who has not experienced it to understand the feeling of freedom when finally driving through that last gate into West Berlin.

So, with joy and apprehension, we made our first trip to West Berlin—our new home in the land where God had called us. We moved into the spacious five-room apartment our predecessor, Thorsten Jahnson, had acquired. Housing in a highly regulated city with virtually no new construction was minimal. He registered it in the church's name, so we could move right in. An additional blessing was that the apartment was visible, barely fifty yards away from the church, across from a small triangular park.

It was 29 years after World War II. Heroically, the people of West Berlin had rid the city of most of the outward scars of the bombs that had destroyed 65 percent of the city's center. As we came to know the Berliners more intimately, we realized that time had not erased the inner scars left.

But God had made us responsible for their spiritual care, and as we won their confidence, they slowly opened and entrusted their stories to us. With others, we also had the privilege of ministering to them in practical ways. As Mary-Esther and I listened to the horrors these dear people had to live through, our hearts would break. Their physical, emotional, and mental injury and pain caused them to erect protective walls within themselves to survive.

However, these are walls that we all erect. Walls our parents teach us. We build walls to protect ourselves from pain and injury of all kinds. These short stories illustrate a few barriers that need to be broken down or overcome.

The Language Barrier and Resentment

Frau Lange came from a wealthy and influential family in Dresden. During the end stages of the war, when the Americans carpet bombed Dresden, she was the only member of her family who was not killed. Her wealth and status were gone, and she moved to Berlin to work as a secretary at the university. Now retired, we would see her spelunking in the trash bins, strolling on the community's sidewalks. Still impacted by the extreme want after the war, she loved to pick through the waste bins for useable things others had discarded. It is not sure when she first started attending, but she stopped coming after our first service. Someone told us others had asked why she had stopped coming. She replied, "Who are they to think they can come over here as Americans and pastor us when they cannot even speak correct German."

For almost a year, Mary-Esther made it a point to engage her in short conversations on the open-air market. It circled the park in front of our apartment twice a week. As Mary-Esther's German improved, Frau Lange slowly warmed up and told Mary-Esther her story. About a year later, she resumed regular attendance. Ultimately, Frau Lange became close to our family. At least once, she gave Mary-Esther a cute skirt. "I found this perfectly nice skirt in a trash can and thought it would look stunning on you." Mary-Esther wore it often. It did look very nice on her.

One Sunday morning, Frau Lange noticed my sermons were in longhand. She approached me slowly.[3] Smiling at me, she asked, "I used to be a rather good typist. If you would like, I could type your sermons." So, she came every Monday morning to type my sermons, just in time to join us for lunch. Sometime later, she told me, "Pastor Kauffman, you have become a real German." It is one of my most cherished compliments. When she was in the hospital near the end of her life, she named Mary-Esther to be the one she wanted to be notified. What a wonderful friend.

Resisting the Help of Others—Generous to a Fault

She had fled for her life with her two children seven times during the war. At least once, she had felt it necessary to start out on foot across Poland with her two small children in a wheelbarrow. Later, she and her children were loaded into a cattle car and transported to an unknown destination. Somehow, they had been able to flee and find their way to West Berlin. After the war, she owned and operated a fish store with a small cafe to feed her family. By the time we knew her, age, and the ravages of life on her own had taken their toll.

She was a poor woman, yet one of the most generous people we have ever known. She regularly brought unsolicited bags of food to church to "fatten up her pastor." We tried many times to dissuade her. Sometimes she lugged them all the way to the parsonage. Our "pride wall" was up, but our salary made what she brought necessary. It was unusual to note that the food stopped coming when we repented our pride.

Forgiveness

Many women in their fifties and sixties told us openly about the second wave of Russian soldiers who came through Berlin. They described the soldiers as bent on avenging the atrocities of the SS-troops had committed against their women in Ukraine and Russia. The soldiers searched for their little sisters and mothers, leaving those who survived their assaults emotionally scarred for life, and plagued with nightmares. There was minimum therapeutic help for their long periods of deep depression and guilt. Their children, our university students, and young professionals were often heirs of those atrocities.

An elderly Christian couple recounted, with tears streaming down their cheeks, how they were tied to chairs in their fourth-story apartment. Then the soldiers made them watch as their three children were tortured and thrown to their deaths from the window. Then they turned to us, smiled sweetly, and told us it had only been through the love of Christ that they had forgiven their tormenters. With God's help, they carried on.

The Separation of LGBTQ+ Prejudice

Peter, a young Jewish man, began attending our services with several of his friends. He told us he was gay, and as best we could determine, his friends were as well. My ministry praxis was unfamiliar with this side of West Berlin. Conventional wisdom was that one in three men had had at least one homosexual encounter. After praying, I determined that I would try to mirror the mind and actions of Jesus. He said in John 3:17 that He had not come to condemn but to rescue. To the woman caught in adultery, *"I do not condemn you, go and sin no more."* Or James, who wrote, *"Mercy triumphs over judgment."*

According to Peter, he had been born within a year of his mother's release from Auschwitz. Apart from the fact that his mother was neither physically nor emotionally healed from the horror she had experienced, he had likely been unexpected and unwanted. He had deep emotional scars which rendered this otherwise intelligent young man incapable of managing life on his own. Because of his emotional and physical fragility, he was often a target and the object of rape. It reached the point where he came to us after an abusive encounter sobbing. We took him into our home where he stayed for several months. We attended to him with love, but he needed a more permanent clinical living situation. While cooperating with his social worker and another pastor in the city, we secured a place in the famous Christian welfare community at Bethel,[4] in Bielefeld, West Germany. Run by the State Church, they provided him with work, his own room, meals, friends, counseling, spiritual ministry, and recreation.

The Walls of Collapsing Buildings

Erich Reichert was born in Berlin when the Nazis came to power. At age 13, he became a member of the Hitler Youth. They quickly singled him out as a leader. When the Allies bombed Berlin, these young teens did the para-military work in the capital city because the troops were on the front. He would run the ridges of the four-story apartment buildings on fire, attempting to save people who might still be in the building. Erich received several citations for his work and twice from Hitler himself. He had been a heroic youngster.

In the 1950s, he had tried a Baptist Church, but being a bit jaded by the hypocrisy he observed, he threw his hands up and swore off "the church." It had been that way for 15-20 years.

When we arrived in 1974, his daughter, Bettina, was attending our church. She studied at the Technical University and often brought her books to church. One day, she forgot to take a critical book home and called me. "Tim, I left a book in the sanctuary. Would you get it for me? My dad will come and pick it up." When he arrived, we made small talk for a short time at the door. While talking, I was praying, "Father, forgive him for his rejection of you and the Church."

Later, Bettina called and exclaimed, "What did you do to my father?" "I just gave him the book, exchanged a few pleasantries, and he left," I replied. She said, "He wants me to make an appointment for him to talk with you."

On my second visit, he accepted Christ into his life. After that, he attended the morning service. He was a tremendous help with the landscaping during the villa's renovation. One day, before the end of the building project, while we were resting on our rakes, he looked at me and said, "I may be older than you, but you are my father." His statement embarrassed and humbled me, but we knew he was referring to earthly and spiritual fatherhood.

Their Stories Need to Be Heard

These are only a few stories of the wonderful people who had suffered a most destructive war. I would often walk in the late evenings along the Kurfürstendamm, the major shopping street in West Berlin. I would also sit at an outdoor café, soak in the atmosphere of the neon lights, and study the thousands of people. Even after midnight, they crowded the wide sidewalks, and I would sit, sip a coffee, and pray for the city and its people. As I would pray, the song "*The Savior is Waiting*" would come to mind, and I would sing it softly to myself: "The Savior is waiting to enter your heart; why don't you let Him come in?" That question was going to take on an even greater significance later. It was the beginning of one of the most incredible adventures of our lives.

Although both times and context may differ, the truths we discovered represent unchanging biblical principles that are universally valid. As we allow Christ to break down our walls of resistance to Him and surrender to His will, He gives us an exciting adventure in return.

The following pages document a selection of the stories of people and situations in which some of the walls we erected needed to be demolished to make His Lordship more complete. The Holy Spirit was behind the scenes working out His perfect will in every situation. As we sought His will and consensus on the church board, He faithfully gifted us with unity of purpose. A culture of mutual love, respect, and deference was evident in the body life of our congregation. I have described all the events recounted according to my best recollection. Only one name, in Chapter 11, did we feel it is necessary to change. Here are their stories.

CHAPTER 2

BIG CONCEPT, BIGGER COLLAPSE

"In his heart, a man plans his course, but the Lord determines his steps." (Proverbs 16:98)

Cultural Arrogance

One of the last things I did before leaving the United States was to participate in a one-week management seminar by Dr. Howard Hendricks. They taught us that good leadership practices include the following four principles: "Plan big—Lead inspiringly—Organize thoroughly—Control faithfully," or (PLOC). It had pretty impressed me with several books on "Positive Thinking." Armed with this information, which might have worked in America, I had crafted a long list of goals for West Berlin before leaving the United States. By the time we arrived, I was burning with a desire to get started.

On a trip to Frankfurt, I met a young evangelist named Hans Jürgen Zimmermann, not long after arriving in West Berlin. He was preaching the Good News to sizeable crowds of youth and seeing many lives changed. He was a talented songwriter/singer and had already cut several albums (cassette tapes back then). Living on a shoestring in a one-room apartment and driving a run-down station wagon someone had given him. He had to believe God for the gas to get him from one meeting to the next. But he was on fire to reach the lost with the message of salvation in Christ and shared my own dreams for ministry. It did not take long for us to start a warm friendship and discuss a revival in West Berlin.

I did not know that in most Germans' minds, setting a huge goal and only achieving half of it amounts to failure.

The church board was utterly unprepared for the furious flurry of possibility thinking, prime goal setting, and management insight descending upon them. It took me twelve months to realize that a German Pietist approach to church does not respond to this leadership style.

Several people, at an appropriate time, left the congregation. The congregation averaged 19 (including children) in those early days on Sunday morning. To lose only a few was a disaster, and we mourned each of them.

I plodded on. That I could push the plans for this mini-Crusade through a reluctant church board showed they were long-suffering with their new "foreign" pastor. We had scheduled Hans-Jürgen Zimmermann as the youth evangelist. We planned a top attendance of 700, a 50-voice choir, and a budget that equaled the giving of the church for the entire previous year.

As I exercised my newly won management skills, I constructed the master plan. I created slots for workers and delineated and delegated tasks (it did not bother me we were too thin on personnel). We sought a hall for 700 people, planned a budget, and paid for advertising. Hans Jürgen would tease me with a chuckle, and jibe me gently, Kauffman, "Du bist verrückt," "You are crazy!" Not until later did it occur to me that he was very definitely right.

Problems developed when we determined that there was no affordable hall for 700 people near enough to rent to say nothing about how much it would cost. The only auditoriums available were too large or too far away. The most significant letdown came when we finally had to have the services in our sanctuary, which seated 100 at a maximum. Even with 100 in attendance, I comforted myself with the thought that to see the church full would be an encouragement for those attending regularly.

The church people did what they could. Despite their pastor's obsessive ideas, they were a brave and faithful group. I think they were all secretly hoping they had misunderstood my extremely poor but improving German. The truth is we were all over-extended by my grandiose plans.

We knocked on over 5,000 doors and hand-delivered invitations to each family. We rented space on the charming cylindrical advertising columns on most European city corners. I displayed the placards we had printed on them in our part of the city. Everyone was exhausted even before we sang the first song.

Hans Jürgen arrived to find an almost hopeless situation. Halfway through the week, several of those who had brought several visitors accused others of being less spiritual because they had only gotten one or two people to come. Those indicted turned on their accusers, calling them overly ambitious. It did not take a prophet to determine that the bickering had its root in my ambition.

The average attendance was 40, with a high of 54. Under normal circumstances, this would have been an excellent result. But the over-ambitious goal setting and the name-calling cost us a few of our regulars. When it was over, the congregation was smaller than in the beginning. I took full responsibility and determined that something like this would never happen again.

Lesson Learned

What had gone wrong was not that we wanted to do something big for the Lord, but that it had been my idea and not His. I had allowed the wall of my desires and cultural insensitivity to come between the hoped-for growth and His plans for achieving it. I had taken off in my own direction and ended up outside Christ's Lordship for this revival. Even though a polite majority vote of the church board was recorded in the minutes to have the meetings in the first place, the direction was wrong. The majority might have the votes, but it does not always have the mind of Christ.

Then, I repented and asked God to help me discover a structure that would bring us together.

CHAPTER 3

BEING "IN ONE ACCORD"

"The more genuine and the deeper our community becomes, the more will everything else between us recede. The more clearly and purely will Jesus Christ and his work become the one and only thing that is vital between us. We have one another only through Christ, but through Christ, we do have one another, wholly, and for all eternity."
Dietrich Bonhoeffer, Life Together

Cultural Insensitivity and Repentance

It is not uncommon for a church board to conflict with its pastor or each other. Given time and familiarity with each other, Christians will exhibit the same or similar behavior in church board sessions as they do at home or at work. A few forceful personalities who are very articulate and opinionated often dominate the conversation in board meetings. Most of the people in the church look to them before they express their own opinions. There are also some temperaments that never seem to get along with others. Such individuals are not beneficial when making group decisions.

When confronted with conflict issues, like we were experiencing, neither pastors nor laypeople will rarely know how to handle them. First, the pastor might resign and allow the dominant people to continue in what usually amounts to narcissistic behavior. Second, the pastor might engage them in a power struggle. If the pastor succeeds, unity is most often destroyed. However, when the pastor leaves, everything returns to normal. A few people are calling the shots, and otherwise capable additional board members have not been included in the decision-making process.

In reflecting on the disastrous revival in April 1975, and after talking to my superior, a picture of how most German people think, and work began to take form in my mind. For example, they are usually very sure of their ground. Once they have thought it over and decided, it is challenging to convince them otherwise. The parliamentary governmental system works with a loyal opposition. A majority vote in a board meeting usually is not enough to win the minority vote to cooperate on a project. Moms and dads teach their children to gather the facts and formulate their own opinions on the issues from a young age. They also instructed them to be able to argue that position well and to modify it only when definitive evidence is introduced. This affects what people do after any vote is taken in Germany.

In Germany, the term "loyal opposition" means just that. They are still loyal but continue to be opposed to the decision. In the extreme, consistency dictates a withdrawal of monetary and moral support from that specific project. When the slightest little setback occurs, the loyal opposition will not hesitate to remind the majority and the voters of its poor decision.

In the United States, democracy means that the majority rules. Everyone supports the vote of the majority, even when one is on the losing side. Even in a close vote, the cooperation of virtually all concerned is assured. This is also true in the American Church.

The West Berlin congregation was very forgiving and kind. However, my leadership style was shaken to the core. It had to change.

My dilemma was how could I be a meaningful pastor in this German context? I had run into the wall at full speed. Something had to give. How could Christ function as the head of His Church when there were such human barriers? How could I accomplish this?

I spent some extra time in prayer and getting quiet before God. The word in German is Stillezeit (quiet time). It did not take long to realize that two things needed to happen to have a unified church where Christ was Lord. First, I would have to change my straight-ahead attitude, and second, the church board would have to make consensus-based decisions.

Stille is the abbreviation for the word used in the Pietist Movement. It is a practice of entering into the presence of God in solitude. The term also includes the idea of spending a longer, more profound, and more specific time in God's presence, seeking a two-way conversation.

During one of those quiet times, in May 1975, the Lord whispered, "Tim, call a 24-hour board meeting and use Stillezeit as the basis for your decision making. Add in the corporate practice of Wesley's sharing around the circle, including all members." That was it! Everyone was approaching God together. Everyone hears from God and expresses it freely in His presence. I hesitatingly explained to the board what I thought the Lord had said, afraid they might object. One board member said he had been thinking the same thing. We reached consensus quickly and prayerfully.

We planned for the board to meet at 5:00 pm on the evening before a national holiday in the larger home of a board member's father, who had made it available. Allow me to explain the agenda of our meeting to assist in describing how we utilized Stillezeit in this larger framework:

5:00 pm   We arrived, got situated in our rooms, freshened up a bit, and had a few minutes to visit.

5:30 pm   The devotional talk was based on the verse in Acts, *"And they were all in one place and in one accord."* Our emphasis was on unity and God's blessing when His people are *"in one accord."* We were all very expectant.

6:30 pm   We fasted the evening meal but set out fruit and fruit drinks for those who needed to eat something. I gave each board member a sheet of paper on which I had the agenda and questions written as prayers. Some questions dealt with our personal lives, and others dealt with the direction of the congregation, past, present, and future. The plan was to integrate these questions into our Stille.

We prayed around the circle just before beginning the first session of three hours of quiet time. Our request was that God would give us the mind of Christ, trusting that He, in the person of the Holy Spirit, was ministering through each of us. We asked that He bind us together in unity and purpose for His Church. We then kept silent for three hours to pray and ask God to speak to us.

This quiet time came at the end of our first evening's deliberations. To avoid any conversations that might taint our conversation with God, we kept absolute silence through the night and breakfast.

7:00 am	Breakfast was a very sacred time. The seven of us and our intern, Ludwig Duncker, ate together around the table. We each attempted to expect each other's needs. We were serving each other without a word.
8:00 am	There were ground rules laid out for our in-session sharing. I gave each person equal time to read aloud or express what he or she believed God had said in the quiet time. No one was to interrupt for any reason. All questions were to be held until all had spoken.
12:00 pm	By noon, everyone had shared once. There had been incredible openness and honesty while sharing our feelings, hopes, and dreams. Yes, some of what they said was hard for me to hear. While they said it in love, I agreed with what they said.
1:00 pm	In the next round, we asked questions for clarification, mentioned points of disagreement, and offered advice or help. By the time we were done, we felt the need to pray for each other, ask forgiveness of each other, counsel, and intercede for each other. God had indeed met with us and joined us into one.
4:00 pm	Taking the notes from all our time together, we took an additional half-hour quiet time to write down the four following right things we felt God wanted to do in the church. We all asked for God's direction in His mission.

4:30 pm	As everyone shared, we tabulated each suggestion on a flip chart. Those items mentioned the most went to the top of the list.
5:00 pm	Our supper together was a celebration. We had indeed become captive of the reality of our oneness in Christ. This time together had truly unified us. Sin and barriers between each other had melted away; the task before us was in view; we had become more convinced than ever that Christ was Lord of His Church.

Now, we looked forward to our board meetings. We made our decisions by consensus. Since then, if we could not agree on a proposal in one session, we would postpone a decision until the next meeting. This gives board members time to rethink their amendments or objections to parts of the proposal. They all know they can continue in their opposition. We voted only in rare cases when one member was unwilling to come to a consensus. This way, the board members realize the pastor was not trying to steamroll his program.

We always found consensus in the next meeting when we considered the issue again. Willingness to compromise strengthens the final product. Everyone's input always betters the product. This manner of working together is possible because we believe Christ is at work in each of us to affect a solution for His Church.

If we are determined to let Christ be the Lord of His Church, we must learn to listen to Him. The exciting thing is that He communicates with us and through us if we will get quiet before Him and give Him time to speak to us. We found that tearing down the walls of our preconceived ideas helped us to focus on His plan and has saved us the time of spinning our wheels or going full speed ahead in the wrong direction.

Lesson Learned

Here are six reasons we found these principles reasonable to follow in our board sessions:

- Some members will not speak up when dominant people are in the group.
- Those who say little very often have the best ideas.
- The adage that is frequently true in the German culture, "once against it, always against it," also applies even if one is not very vocal.
- We squelch some of the best ideas before they have a chance because someone says, "That can never work." With this procedure, all opinions have an equal opportunity to be heard because they are all on the table before anyone can criticize them.
- If everyone is in on a decision and has "equal time" for input, it is easier to reach a consensus. This process also helps the more dominant on the board come to respect those more introverted and realize the Holy Spirit is speaking through them, as well.
- Total ownership of goals on a church board results from consensus. The strength of the board's unity flows into the congregation. Knowing Christ is leading lends tremendous power because everyone is working towards the same goal.

The theological basis of this spiritual exercise is that:

- Prayer should not be a one-way street.
- We cannot be aware of God's still small voice if we do not deliberately take time to get quiet and listen.
- Our prayers are usually a long litany of requests with no time to concentrate on God Himself.
- All these factors and many more represent barriers to effective communication with God. We often register surprise when someone mentions that God said this or that to them. "Can God speak to us today?"

God will speak to us in ways we can be sure of if we take the time to quiet ourselves and meditate on Him alone. Prayer is a time when God is more interested in talking with us than we are in speaking with Him. The secret is to remain quiet before Him until we are confident that we have heard from Him.

He knows our needs and the things hurting us before we ask. If we have requests, He delights in our bringing them to Him. When He speaks words of encouragement, all our minor problems and fears become insignificant. When He assures us that our needs are met, we can only praise Him. This comes remarkably close to what the old-timers called "praying through."

It is all important that the pastor and the board listen to God's voice in the silence of His presence. Some might fear that "visionaries" may take over such a situation. There is always that danger. The principle is that every board member knows how to speak up, and no one can decide alone. It becomes more difficult for one individual to influence a board when it is already a unit and has procedures to deal with such attempts.

CHAPTER 4

BEING MUTUALLY TRANSPARENT

"With genuine confession, everything can be healed; without confession, nothing can be healed." (Tim Keller)

Confession of Faults

Some of the highest walls loom in our relationships. This is true when it happens between those responsible for the spiritual welfare of a congregation. They often include wrongful attitudes like envy, resentment, and bearing grudges that remain hidden and can hinder Christ's love from flowing unhindered in our relationships.

In January 1976, about twelve adults and children attended the church retreat in Mönchberg, the Retreat Center in West Germany. The retreat house was in a small village in a medium mountain range. It had been snowing so hard that we almost did not make it up the mountain.

We had been in Germany for almost two years, and I still felt frustrated with my ability to communicate in the German language. It was as though the man inside me sounded like a twelve-year-old child when he opened his mouth. I had relied significantly on Werner Zimmermann, our lay leader, who was an excellent and articulate Bible teacher. I was grateful to have him, but I was envious of his facility with the language as he would interpret the Scriptures. All the people looked to him for advice and leadership.

So, here we were, together for a week without TV or radio. The Lord had led me to use the book of 1 John for our devotional times. However, as I came to the passage about loving your brother, the Holy Spirit spoke to me about my feelings toward Werner. The Holy Spirit uncovered how I had secretly become resentful of

Werner's advantage with the language. I had felt threatened by the authority of his teaching, and his ability to communicate with the church people. And God convicted me to confess it to Werner and ask him to forgive me.

It took a day or two before I could muster up my courage. Finally, after lunch, I approached him about taking a walk in the woods. The Germans love to take extended walks after lunch on weekends and holidays, and Werner readily joined me. It had snowed again during the night, and the trees glistened with a blanket of white glory. Even the paths were trackless. We left the house and made our way up the trail. Since we were friends and there was nothing objectively wrong with our relationship, it was difficult for me to find a lead-in for my apology. I exclaimed about the pristine beauty of the new snow, and we exchanged small talk. My hands became increasingly clammy in my gloves as the walk proceeded, even on that cold wintery afternoon. My heart was racing. When we were back in sight of the house, Finally, I could no longer hold it in.

I stopped, turned to him, and told him of how the Lord had been speaking to me over the past few days. I then confessed how inadequate and resentful of his great gift I had felt over the past eighteen months and asked him to forgive me. Werner expressed surprise and told me he was unaware of such feelings. "I forgive you," he said. Then Werner acknowledged harboring similar feelings toward me. The breadth of my liberal arts education allowed me to talk intelligently with all the students about their studies. He, too, asked forgiveness, which I instantly granted.

That day was the basis for an even more fruitful and harmonious partnership and complete trust in each other. I would drive to his photography store and spend half an hour between customers discussing church issues. We dreamed together, made plans, and bounced ideas and strategies off each other. We gave each other additional time to think about our proposals. There was never any lost prestige if we did not agree.

Leaders Need to Work Together

Friendship or not, pastors and lay leaders must learn to work together. God's Kingdom's work is based on His people's prayerful collaboration. The walls of self-interest, influence peddling, and petty pride in leadership will hinder inner spiritual growth and influence the congregation. God is interested in the continuity of spiritual care of the community. We fight spiritual battles with spiritual weapons. If cooperation seems impossible, the first task is prayer and fasting. What a pastor pushes through against the lay leader[5] will not likely last long after the pastor is gone.

To say it positively, the pastor who can form a fruitful working relationship with the lay leaders in the church will accomplish much that will last. Pastoring a unified congregation will have a lasting spiritual impact on a church long beyond that pastor's tenure.

The Lord had answered my prayer and had given me at least a partial answer to my quest. Nine months had passed, but the groundwork for Christ's Lordship in our working together for His Kingdom's sake was firmly laid. Waiting on Christ and asking for forgiveness were the main pillars of this bulwark.

Werner Zimmermann

Werner was the owner of a small but flourishing camera store in a shopping center about five miles from the city's center. The congregation acknowledged him as their lay leader.

Since then, he has sold his business and founded nationwide management and vocational consulting firms. In addition, he and his wife have become nationally known nutrition experts. Werner told me what the small Nazarene congregation in West Berlin has meant to him.

> "Were I to describe in one word what life in the Schmargendorf Church meant to me, it would be hope. Everyone who came into the church for any reason experienced this hope, too. Some of the most important biblical principles in the church's life were: 1) the preaching--based on God's Word, 2) each

member--determined to live out the Lordship of Christ, and 3) accountability in fellowship with one another.

"Never in my life was I so aware of how much we need the fellowship and support of others. How wonderful the candid conversations we had, how uncomplicated it was getting along with each other. What joy sitting together for hours sharing personal experiences and thinking through theological issues.

"The worship experience was a high point for all of us. After the service, no one was in a hurry to leave. The fellowship and the conversations after the service showed that we were comfortable in each other's presence. We learned that fellowship with each other is fellowship with our Lord. We received encouragement, joy, and the hope of Christ's return through giving.

"In the quality of our life together, I see encouragement for the people of our industrial civilization. It is a place where families can find healing in an atmosphere of faith and caring. There is no alternative to the church's ministry within the Lordship of Christ. Nothing else rebuilds people, develops their personalities, and gives them refuge without manipulating and using them.

"One of the most critical parts of life is a church under the Lordship of Christ. Occasionally, I would taste the breath of heaven. I wanted to capture it, hold it close, and revel in it. Such moments are Christ's gift to us. They are unique. They do, however, point us to the Lordship of Christ and the Hope He represents. That is why I'm so thankful for these years together."

Lessons Learned

Three human components are essential in a harmonious working relationship in the Church of Christ: 1) the pastor, 2) the lay leader, and 3) the church board.

In every congregation, there is someone to whom everyone turns when they have a question or when they disagree with a pastoral or a board decision. This person has gatekeeper status, whether he or she has an elected position. Even if a pastor successfully maneuvers him or her out of elected office, that person will still have power outside the elected office.

These three components are like three circles within Christ's Lordship. The more concentric they become, the greater their effectiveness in growth within the church. If any of the circles decide it does not want to move toward the others, then the power declines.

When the walls of self-interest, petty pride, the desire to be correct, and many more go up, Christ's leadership in a church suffers. Only after much soul searching and the certainty that the principle is guiding one's position should one dare challenge the unity of the group. The case when Paul challenged the Jerusalem Council about requiring Gentile Christians to adhere to the Jewish law is a case in point. The truth is usually convincing.

CHAPTER 5

THE STEPS TOWARD SELF-SUPPORT

"Because of the service by which you have proved yourselves, men will praise God for the obedience that accompanies your confession of the gospel of Christ. And for your generosity in sharing with them and with everyone else." (II Corinthians 9:13)

The Wall of Self-Preservation

An important test of the Lordship of Christ in our personal lives and the church is to what extent we have removed the wall of self-preservation and given Christ control of our finances. Considering the average income of a congregation, household giving in almost any community can tell a great deal about the quality of Christ's Lordship.

One of the new goals was to increase the level of our giving. To help our church encourage increased dependence on the Lord and pull together toward a worthy goal, we started a modest remodeling project on the building. Another thing we discussed in our long board meeting was the need to keep goals attainable. Giving tends to stabilize at the same level after the project is over. In a healthy growing church, it may even continue to increase. Because they have experienced the joy of giving, healthy Christians are not nearly as protective of their pocketbooks. Also, it is especially important to note that in a culture of consensus, the power of unity and goal ownership is an integral factor in giving.

Our first project was the renovation of the inside of the church. We decided what we wanted to do, estimated how much it would cost, and presented it to the church membership. We needed to raise $2,000, or DM 4,500 over six months.[6]

THE STEPS TOWARD SELF-SUPPORT

The board approved it and pitched in with great gusto. Some new young people were good at wallpapering and laying carpet. God gave us some beautiful evenings of fellowship. Several of these new people fully integrated into the church through this project.

However, this was just a warm-up for the goal of becoming self-supporting. Our church was paying its own bills, but my salary was still coming from the district since we were on a mission project.

Self-Support Is Reachable

The district was still subsidizing our operating costs with funds designated for new church starts. One evening in January, after closing the books for the fiscal year 1974, we analyzed the church's giving records, and noticed that giving increased 20% in 1974. If we could raise in advance $6,000 in special giving, put it in the bank, and have a 20% increase in our annual giving over the next two years, by 1976 the church could be self-supporting.

The plan was to use the $6,000 in the bank to create a cushion we could use in 1975 to supplement our increased giving in 1975. And then again, in faith, to declare ourselves self-supporting at the District Assembly in 1976.

The board prayed about this proposal and voted unanimously to do it. We then presented it to the congregation:

Since we had already raised $2,000 in six months to fix up the building, we believed, with God's help, to raise $6,000 in a year to be self-supporting.

We were not giving for ourselves, but freeing up what was being given to us to support future churches. Our horizons needed to be broadened. This project would strengthen our faith for the future and perhaps even more daunting projects later. We made our pledges over the time of one year.

After a short discussion in a church meeting, we took pledges and reached our goal of $6,000 that morning. As the months went by, the church's giving, and growth continued to stay on course. By the end of 1975, we had $6,000 in the bank. Was our regular income going to increase to $33,000 in the '75-'76 fiscal year as well? Here is where our faith really needed to take hold. We were going to declare ourselves self-supporting a year early at the District Assembly, trusting that it would happen.

We asked an artist in the church to draw an oversized check on posterboard. We presented it to Rev. Richard Zanner during my report to the district. It was a great blessing for those Berliners who made the seven-hour trip from West Berlin to Frankfurt. From that moment on, we received no more financial help from the district.

The End of the Story

By March of 1977, we had used up our cushion, but the level of our giving had also increased. At the end of the fiscal year, the balance in the fund was $60.00. Increased giving was based on growing the congregation, not asking the same people to give more. Both the giving and the widening ministry grew steadily.

Lessons Learned

Christ must be the Lord of our personal pocketbooks and the finances of the congregation if He is to be Lord of His Church. Obedience in giving at this stage in God's forming us was crucial for what He was planning later.

The walls of self-preservation must fall and become bridges of self-sacrifice and service. "He who will save his life will lose it, and he who loses his life for my sake will find it" (Matthew 10:39). When Christ is Lord, He will always direct us to active concern for others. Serving individuals and/or peoples outside our immediate sphere of influence will pulsate with the excitement and adventure only Christ's Spirit can bring. When Christ becomes the Lord of our finances, it is a considerable step toward His complete Lordship in our lives.

To discover how a majority vote and His will can be synonymous in a German cultural context, the walls erected by my plans, which I had expected Him to bless, would have to be torn down. I was going to wait for Him. Everything would have to be planned at His initiative and with His involvement. Exactly how this was supposed to happen at this time and in this place, I did not yet know. It had driven me to my knees and became a regular part of my quiet time in the morning before the Lord. But the search had begun.

PART II
CHRIST'S FAITHFULNESS AS LORD

CHAPTER 6

MINISTRY TO FAMILIES

"Father and Mother are apostles, bishops and priests to their children, for it is they who make them acquainted with the gospel." — Martin Luther

The Wall of Dysfunction

One of the most exciting outgrowths of our 24-hour board meeting was the idea of starting a family ministry. In the beginning, outside of our family, there was only Werner Zimmermann's family of five.

We believed that too many homes in West Berlin were experiencing a wall of dysfunction in some form. Even then, Christian families struggled with the cultural influences that made it challenging to live out the Lordship of Christ as a family at home.

Therefore, if Christ is to be Lord of our lives and His Church, His Lordship must also be visible in our homes. This conviction gave birth to our ministry to families.

In contemplating methods of winning new people to Christ in Germany, we considered the fact that Sunday is a family day. Virtually all the retail stores are closed, and other businesses would come to a virtual halt from Saturday at 1:00 pm until Monday morning. Because children often had school on Saturday morning, the time for the family to do something together was Sunday. In addition, the father usually still had the last word with decisions about family activities.

As soon as a German couple had their first child, they would most often stop attending because the State Church has minimal facilities to care for babies or small children. Adding the fact that mothers found it challenging to give their newborns (up to 18 months) into the care of others, one could see a considerable hindrance to new young families.

Women over the age of 50 predominantly attend the state churches of Germany. As soon as the children are old enough to attend church, their mom might take them to the children's church, which runs concurrently with the church service. As soon as the children reach the age of 16, they take confirmation classes. After confirmation, most of them stop attending. This leaves mom there alone until the grandchildren come along.

Particularly unreached by the church are working-class husbands. They have other activities on Sunday morning: hobbies, doting on their cars, a family hike in the nearby woods or landscape, sports club participation (Germany organizes all sports around clubs), or talking politics in a local bar.

We concluded that the best way to win families was to reach the fathers first. If we could win dad, his choice would be decisive as to what the family's Sunday morning activity would be. The mom, who is most often already interested, will seldom object.

Being only two families at first, we worked together with the Zimmermanns. They were a vital part of the establishing process. With unity of purpose and the church board unified behind the effort, we directed all our energies into the project.

How We Got Started

The four of us met and strategized about how we might proceed. We prayed around the circle and then continued to work through a sequence of activities:

We listed those families we thought might be interested in taking part. They needed a positive stance on the Bible and the local church.

Before we contacted anyone, we covenanted to pray for each family daily for a month and asked God to show us who we should contact first. It was important to pray as a couple or as a family if the children were old enough.

We invited each prospective family (one at a time) to our place for supper. After supper, we explained what we were praying about and hoping to accomplish together.

We continued this process until we had 4-5 additional families willing to try it out. It was important for continued success to have initial families who were most likely to attend the meetings regularly.

We set a date for the first meeting. At our first meeting, we took time to brainstorm about topics we felt were important or needed in our family life.

Some Topics We Came Up With

Depending on the topic, we sometimes separated into men's and women's groups.

- Generation problems and communication.
- Overcoming our past.
- The place of punishment as correction and self-discipline in raising children.
- Handling the use of the mass media at home.
- Dealing with neighbors.
- The goals of Christian marriage.
- Ways to enhance the romance in one's union.
- Forgiveness is a principle in living together successfully.
- Possibilities for family activities.
- A free day for Mom each month.
- School—healthy and unhealthy friendships.
- Money and household planning.

Time Schedule

3:00-3:45	Coffee, cake, fellowship, and conversation.
3:45-4:15	A group member spoke briefly on the day's subject. We all took turns. Training for new leaders for later.
4:15-4:45	We considered how the talk would be about their marriage and family life in Stille.
4:45-5:45	We shared what we had written. We all gave and took counsel from one another.

5:45-6:00   We had a prayer fellowship and set the date of the next meeting.

Our meetings rotated from home to home. The host family often babysat (we usually had teenagers or grandparents who took the children on a walk to a park or played with them in another room. The plan was to divide into two groups during the summer to prepare for the fall's expansion.

These families, even the children, enjoyed this enriching fellowship. The children formed fast friendships with children of Christian families. Even those who were not yet Christians did not want to miss. Sharing openly with others who had the same problems and looking for solutions together was a great encouragement for families feeling hard-pressed by today's world. The most significant difficulty was that the families would become so close they would not want to divide the group. Thus, we emphasized our responsibility to pass our experiences on to others.

Lessons Learned

Our prayer at first was that the Lord would help us to have five new families in regular attendance by the end of the year. At the end of that year, we had six. This encouraged us to ask for 20 families. By the time we moved into our villa-church on Grunewald Ave., there were three groups with five or six families in each group and over 20 families in church attendance.

Neglect, unkindness, or bitterness are walls often placed brick by brick between marriage partners, parents, and children. Slowly put into place over the years between individuals, Neglect can present a formidable barrier to Christ's Lordship in the congregation. But families who live and interact with each other according to scriptural principles are the foundation of a solid Christian community.

CHAPTER 7

MENTORING LEADERS

"Has the community served to make individuals free, strong, and mature or has it made them insecure and dependent? Has it taken them by the hand for a while so that they would learn again to walk by themselves, or has it made them anxious and unsure?"— Dietrich Bonhoeffer, Life Together and Prayerbook of the Bible

The Wall of Inaccessibility

One would think that in a walled city, there would not be a problem with ease of access to the church. It did not take long to notice that even though our church was in the city's center, the wall of inaccessibility loomed high. Some families responding to our ministry lived as far away as a 45-minute drive from the church. With their irregular schedules, many of our students and young professionals lived far enough away to make only Sunday morning attendance possible. The attendance on Sunday evenings, with the afterglow in the parsonage, was smaller. Still, Wednesday evening Bible Study attendance was more meager.

Why not transform a problem into an opportunity? By the end of 1976, I shared with Werner my idea of taking the prayer meeting time on Wednesday evening to the people. He was immediately interested. The plan was to select and train three lay people to take over three Bible studies in their respective parts of the city. The church board was also unanimous in trying it. We made plans.

The group of leaders met every other week on Saturday afternoon for just one hour. If we were to open Home Bible Studies in three or four places with clusters of congregants, we could have a much more significant spiritual impact on the daily lives of our lay people.

There were at least five ways, it seemed to me, the idea of restructuring the Wednesday evening experience would build up these new believers:

a. In reading the history of the Pietistic Movement in Germany, we saw that minor Home Bible Studies were indigenous and culturally appropriate.
b. I would have the privilege of mentoring the Home Bible Studies and leaders.
c. By eliminating the driving distances people needed to travel to church on Wednesday evening, people could invite nearby friends and acquaintances to attend.
d. In a more intimate small group, individuals in the church can form strong bonds and foster more profound and accountable discipleship. These qualities are necessary to create a cohesive Christian community, which cannot happen on Sunday morning only.
e. We were already praying for and dreaming of planting a second church somewhere in West Berlin and beginning a compassionate ministry. Growing Bible Studies on the city's periphery would increase the possibility in the future.

Thus, in May 1977, we began three new Bible studies in three different parts of the city. Each Home Bible Study had a layperson (preferably local to the venue) as its leader and an assistant. We accomplished several things founding the Bible Studies:

The number of those attending and growing in their faith on Wednesday evenings doubled at first. And it kept increasing as time went on.

We had launched outposts in three parts of the city, any of which could become a second church. We prayed God would bless and multiply the groups.

Each attendee could grow in an accountability atmosphere within a small group environment. Our new converts got personal spiritual help and grew more substantial in the Lord.

Considering the city's geopolitical uncertainty, this move would enhance our future flexibility. If the time ever came when the church could not function normally, we would have recourse.[7]

We prayed that each Bible Study would develop its individual dynamic in growth and evangelism. Then, were it to become a new church start, it would already have learned how to grow and multiply naturally. The seeds and lessons of bearing fruit would already be in place.

Multiplication

About a year after we began the Bible studies, one leader, Tomas Rosenhalm, came to my office. He told me that God was talking with him about starting a fourth Bible study in his apartment in the southern part of the city. He explained that his assistant leader, the family's husband where his Bible study met, could take over as leader. The groups had grown and would accept this idea if we decided favorably.

I said I thought it was a great idea but wanted to pray about it and talk it over with the church board. This conversation was a huge confirmation that God was answering our prayers and that the destruction of the wall of inaccessibility was bearing eternal fruit. Standing in front of the city map on the wall in our hallway, I mused, "Who knows, Tomas? Maybe the Lord wants to start a new church in Lichtenrade."

After getting the green light, Tomas Rosenhalm set to work. It grew until there was no more room in their living room to hold the meetings. Thomas Vollenweider, our new assistant pastor, and his wife, Esther, had come to Berlin to help us start a second church. In praying with them, we decided they should begin an additional Bible study in the living room of another family in Lichtenrade. These Bible studies became the nucleus of the second church in West Berlin – the Jakobusgemeinde (St. James Church).

The benefits of starting Bible studies on Wednesday evening were clear. The attendance had grown. New Christians had found a place to grow in the faith. And as a small community with lay leadership development, we started a second church in West Berlin.

Mentoring the Lay Leaders

My role in this endeavor was to train the leaders on a rotating schedule. The key to this new structure working was mentoring the lay leadership.

We also met every third week after the Sunday evening service in my office for two hours. We would talk about how each of them was doing spiritually from several perspectives. There were six of them, four leaders and two assistants. One or two had their own curriculum, and we would discuss it and then prep the others on Bible studies I had prepared for them. In that confidential setting, we helped each other. We asked each other questions like those in John Wesley's society meetings. We grew together in a circle of mutual love and respect.

- Is your prayer life current?
- Where are you having personal spiritual problems?
- How deep can you take your people spiritually?
- What have you been using for study material?
- Do you serve refreshments? How much? When?
- Do you still enjoy being a Bible Study leader?
- What can we do for you to help you become a better leader?

I stressed that one can only give on Wednesday evening what one has received in personal devotions and preparation during the previous week. You would think that adults in the modern age of personal freedoms would balk at being grilled about their spiritual lives in front of their peers. With our group, however, the opposite was true. If one or the other leader expressed a spiritual need, we would gather around them, lay hands on them, and pray for their specific needs. We provided an atmosphere of mutual love and prayer support, and within those parameters, everyone flourished. No one ever missed a meeting. It was not unusual for someone to get up out of a sick bed to be there. They became effective lay leaders. As they were ready, I taught three of them how to prepare and deliver sermons. They would preach their sermons in front of me, an audience of one, and then we would debrief afterward.

Lessons Learned

Bringing down the wall of isolation opened new possibilities for the Gospel's penetration. It made it possible for our little congregation to have a more significant impact as leaven, salt, and light in our city. For us, it meant: 1) lowering the threshold for first-time attendees by meeting in neutral facilities, 2) concentrating on mentoring lay leaders, and 3) leaving it up to Christ's direction as to where new Home Bible Studies and eventually a new congregation would be located.

Mentoring Future Pastors

Our Bible College's curriculum stipulated their students spend eight weeks of practicum (internship) in a church setting. Most students broke it down to two four-week sessions during their summer break. During our time in West Berlin, some of the most meaningful times we experienced were that month in the summer with student interns.

What Happens During an Internship?

Besides Thomas and Esther, others were with us for a one-month experience to discover what being a pastor involved: Karsten Köplin, Ludwig Dunker, Monika Lau, Ulf Weisensee, and Wolfgang Bauert. One of the most essential parts of an internship was that the students would spend quite a significant amount of time with the pastor. So, in the morning at 6:00 am, we would meet for one hour for personal devotions in my home office. We would each spend part of that hour in personal Stille with God and the Scriptures.

Then, for example, in the first week I visited, they would tag along, and after the visit, we would debrief. As time passed, I gave the interns increasing responsibility until they could do a few visits themselves, then debrief. I once took Thomas in the middle of the night to prevent someone from committing suicide. Ludwig took part in the entire and important all-day board meeting. They preached once in the month of their stay, taught a Sunday school class, and were active in all the church's auxiliaries. They also attended board meetings. Several of the interns attended our day-long board meetings with Stillezeit. They visited hospitals and the elderly, helped with the youth group, the newsletter, etc. It was a typical internship where we exposed them to the pastor's ministry. Thomas and I laughed, cried, worked, prayed together, and felt an immediate affinity for each other. Mary-Esther and Esther felt like sisters by the time the month was over.

The Long-Term Impact of Mentoring[8]

Thomas, once one of my interns, wrote to me about his experience in the mentoring process.

"This also applies to taking on interns you started, and I could continue! The career of these young people shows us how important these times as interns are for our vocational and spiritual formation":

- Ludwig Duncker, your second intern, became your successor in the Grunewald congregation.
- Thomas Vollenweider was the founding pastor of the St. James congregation. He served as District Superintendent of the Churches in Germany for 20 years and pastored the Lydia congregation. When Thomas became established, he continued mentoring others.
- Ingo Hunaeus (Thomas mentored the rest) became the pastor in Wiesbaden and Seligenstadt. He is now District Superintendent of the Churches in Germany
- Wolfgang Schwarzfischer became Thomas' successor at the St. James Church. He has now been the pastor of the Hügelstrasse congregation in Frankfurt am Main (the Mother Church) for 10 years.

- Martin Wahl became the founding pastor of the Saint John Church. He was District Superintendent of the churches in Germany for eight years and is now the Director of Northern Germany (Berlin/Hamburg)."

Lessons Learned

Whether mentoring future pastors or laypeople, the key is accessibility to someone known to be an experienced practitioner in what you want to learn. I believe the apostle Paul is also speaking about the mentoring process in 2 Timothy 2: 2 "And the things you have heard me say in the presence of many witnesses entrust to reliable people who will also be qualified to teach others." God has given me the gift of seeing my life verse played out for me. Pastors can uniquely reproduce themselves and pass their abilities on to trusted persons who will do the same for additional workers in the harvest. Anything that isolates trusted followers of Christ from finding their full spiritual potential in the congregation must come down.

CHAPTER 8

GOD WILL WATCH OVER THAT WHICH BELONGS TO HIM

> *"You sympathized with those in prison and joyfully accepted the confiscation of your property because you knew that you yourselves had better and lasting possessions. So do not throw away your confidence; it will be richly rewarded."*
> *(Hebrews 10:34-35)*

The Wall of Our Possessions

Why does it seem that the most generous people I know are those who have little to nothing? Their giving is most often spontaneous. Their possessions do not represent a wall built out of the fear of having nothing. It is told in the New Testament about how the first Christians practiced spontaneous giving. This trait was the product of the Holy Spirit and the Lordship of Christ in the believers.

As our possessions increase, sometimes they can own us, and we can erect a wall between them and our generosity. When we submit ourselves to the Lordship of Christ, all we have is no longer ours. It belongs to Christ. All barriers to protect our possessions must come down.

Before we left for Europe, we attended a seminar where someone said something I have never forgotten. It was, "God can, and will, take care of that which belongs to Him." This principle has become linked to our theological underpinning for Mary-Esther and me. It has become a vital part of our daily lives. Everything we have belongs to Him and is at His disposal to be used at His discretion. The result has been nothing short of sheer adventure and events bordering on the miraculous.

We had been in Berlin for only a few months. They were hard months of getting acclimated, learning the language, struggling to preach in German, and attempting to pastor simultaneously. I had lost 30 precious pounds and was feeling anemic. Mary-Esther finally persuaded me to go to the hospital for tests. After three days of non-stop testing, the only thing the doctors found was an overactive, acidic stomach.

I had been out of the hospital only a few days when Monika Lau, our missionary President in nurses' training, stopped by the house. Since we were just sitting down for supper, we invited her to eat with us. As we ate, she mentioned a young man on her floor had been there for several weeks with a mysterious illness. It puzzled the doctors about where it had come from. And they could not treat him. She told us he was alone in Berlin and would soon be discharged with no place to go. She asked if I would visit him.

Ministering to Michael

A few days later, I took a layperson and drove to the hospital. It was a large university teaching hospital a few miles away with over 2,000 beds. After searching for over an hour, we finally found Michael. We talked to him about his illness and then about the Lord. After reading the "Four Spiritual Laws," he prayed and accepted Christ. We then instructed him further, prayed for his healing, and left. Later, we learned that his symptoms had disappeared overnight, as uncannily as they had come. They released him from the hospital the next day. Since he did not have a place to stay, it seemed logical for us to take him in until he found a tiny one-room apartment and a job.

We picked him up at the hospital on a Sunday afternoon. He was driven to a street meeting we were conducting on the Kurfürstendamm (the famous and fashionable shopping street in West Berlin) to prepare for the evening service. Several people asked about attending. We drove to the church from the Kurfürstendamm, a short drive from there, with several new people who had accepted our invitation. Because new people were in attendance, we asked Michael to give a brief testimony. We were all very moved by his simple but powerful witness.

We spent a great deal of time trying to find an apartment and a job for Michael, but it was much more complicated than we had envisioned. He was fun to have around. I remember playing with him and John David, our young son, in the hallway for more than an hour at a time with a super ball. It was great fun.

He had been with us for three weeks, and there seemed no end. This did not bother us greatly, and we were far from being discouraged about it.

The VW Bus is Gone

One evening, Michael seemed restless and very uptight. When I asked him what was wrong, he said his mother in Hamburg was extremely sick. He asked if he could borrow the VW bus, which belonged to the church, to visit her over the weekend. I replied that the train would be cheaper and quicker. After calling a friend to borrow the money, Michael asked if he could borrow the bus to get the money. I reluctantly gave him the keys, but I never dreamed he would double-cross me. We waited well into the night, but he did not return.

Not knowing the legal situation, I called Rev. Zanner, my superior. He advised us to go to the police station and report the stolen bus if we wanted to have any claim on insurance money. With a heavy heart, I went to the police station the following day and told the sergeant that Michael, our houseguest, had stolen the church bus.

The church people took it better than we could have expected. They did not even scold us for our naivete, even though most must have thought it. We encouraged each other to pray that we somehow get the bus back. Remembering that the bus belonged to God, we were sure He would take care of it. Neighbors and friends who did not yet believe also asked what we would do. I said to them with total assurance, "It is God's bus. He can take care of His property. He'll either help us get it back or He will have something better."

In the meantime, we had discovered that the bus was not the only thing he had taken. Three or four days later, I went to the bank to pick up some cash. The lady at the counter gave me my bank statement; I noticed a canceled 1,000 DM ($450) missing from my checkbook. Michael had taken one of my checks and forged it badly. We were 1,000 DM poorer. We had to make do.

The local branch in West Germany had followed none of the prescribed rules to pay a check made out to cash. First, German bank law allowed a cash payout of only 250 DM.

Second, the presenter of any check made out to cash must produce a passport to validate the signature. They followed neither protocol. I had recourse. So, I filled out an insurance claim at the bank. However, they gave me no assurances they would return anything.

A day later, we also discovered that the movie camera Mary-Esther and I had given each other as a wedding present was gone. That was an even greater shock than the missing money. Our son John was not yet three, and we wanted to film some memories. Yet we were still determined to keep it all in God's hands.

The Bus is Back!

Three weeks passed, and there was no word from the authorities. On Saturday night, around 10:00 pm, the telephone rang. A restaurant owner in West Germany was on the line. He asked me if a young man named Michael was legitimately driving a bus registered in the church's name. Michael, he continued, maintains we had loaned the bus to him. I answered I recorded the bus with the police as stolen and that they were looking for it. He agreed to call the police station. A few minutes later, the police called and told us we could pick up the bus. They gave me directions on how to get there and made an appointment for Monday at 10:00 am

The next morning in church was a day of rejoicing. But the genuine adventure was just beginning. After the evening service, I took the night train to Heidelberg, where my good friend Alfred Schaar, a pastor in Stuttgart, picked me up. He was late because of snow showers. I hopped in the car and headed to the town where we had been told the bus was located. It was quite a long drive and took longer than expected. Because of spring rains, the Neckar River had covered the road, and they directed us on a detour through a small town.

My friend apologized because we were late. He was upset. To make matters worse, we had to drive through this one-light town. We were already late because of the snow; sitting at the village's only red light in a small village, we were far off our route. There was no way we would have ever been there on our own. I had just reassured Alfred that God had given me peace about the whole thing. Scarcely had I finished the sentence when Michael, of all people, popped around the corner and disappeared into the corner building. I could not believe my eyes. All I could do was stammer, "Th-there he is!"

"There is who?" Alfred asked.

"The man who took the bus," I exclaimed. At that moment, it occurred to me we had just passed a police station, and we turned around, drove to the station, and informed them of what we had experienced. They followed us to the corner building, but we saw Michael walking toward us on the sidewalk. We persuaded him to get into the police car and drove back to the police station. While there, I told him we had forgiven him but that our seeing each other should prove that he could not run away from God.

I asked him about the movie camera and the check. He admitted to taking the camcorder but claimed someone had stolen it from him. As far as the money was concerned, he was afraid to drive the bus without seat belts and had spent two-thirds of it on new seat belts and a new radio. The police could not hold him but told us that he was already under indictment for several other crimes. So, as suddenly as God had led us together, our ways parted. We drove on to our appointment.

The bus was no longer at that station but in Ulm, about 150 km away. My friend did not have time to drive me to Ulm, so he took me to the train station and offered to let me stay at his place in Stuttgart, since the process would take place later into the evening. I took up Alfred's offer to let me stay at his residence.

I took a taxi from the train station to the police station, arriving at closing time. Sure enough, the bus was standing in the parking lot. After I identified myself, the clerk gave me the keys. While inspecting it, there was indeed a new radio and seatbelts. When I turned the key, the motor did not start. I popped the hood and saw someone had separated the gas line from the carburetor. I fixed that quickly, but the engine still had no life. It was the rotor that was missing. The police motor pool was closed, as were the VW dealers. Seeing visions of having to sleep in the sub-freezing bus all night with no blankets, I rushed back to the clerk to ask where I might locate a rotor.

"There may be someone in the motor pool. Look back there," he replied. So, I returned. Someone was there this time.

"Could you help me? I need a rotor for my VW-bus carburetor."

"I do not work here," he answered. "I just came in to look for something. The only place I know where to get a rotor for a '69 VW-bus is at a VW dealer."

"I'm from out of town. The VW dealer is closed, and I only have enough for gas money back to Berlin. Are you sure there is no other place open?"

"Just a minute!" he proclaimed. "I think I have a rotor in my toolbox. I do not know if it will fit on your bus. We can try it."

Outside, he opened the trunk of his car, pulled out a cardboard box, and rooted around in it. Finally, I saw him hold up a part that looked familiar. "Here it is," he said. We went to the back of the bus, set it on the distributor, and put the cap back on. I turned the ignition key, praying as I did. The motor sprang to life without the slightest hesitation. I asked the good Samaritan if I could give him anything for the rotor. He replied, "You'll need a meal on the road back to Berlin."

Praising God for the memorable day, I drove a VW bus with a new radio, rotor, and front safety belts to Stuttgart. Reflecting on the day's happenings and the wonder of it all, it hit me that Michael could have been anywhere in Germany that morning. It was as though God had directed us to where he was. I have never shaken the thought that God must have something for that young man to do. That was God's timing!

Lessons Learned

As I have mentioned, Michael had put 650 DM into the bus using the $1,000 DM check he had forged. When the next Christmas came around, we wondered how we would finance our Christmas shopping. I went to the bank to pick up the monthly food money. The bank manager approached me with a big smile and gave me a deposit slip. He said, "I thought you might like to see this." There, I saw a deposit of 1,000 DM in our account. It was the insurance money! I had forgotten, but God had not.

The bus was back! It was running better than ever. It had 650 DM of improvements, and the bank had returned 1,000 DM. The seat belts and radio were free. The wall of ownership can come down, and an additional dimension of trust can develop. Christ can do miraculous things if we will relinquish our rights. He really CAN take care of that which belongs to Him!

CHAPTER 9

A TIN CAN AND GOD'S PROVISION

"And God is able to make all grace abound to you, so that in all things at all times, having all that you need, you will abound in every good work." (II Corinthians 9:8)

The Wall of Language

Before we began our ministry in Berlin, I knew very little German. Mary-Esther came to Germany with absolutely no background in the language. After a seven-week course at Goethe Institute, we moved to West Berlin. She was doing exceptionally well, but had no experience in conversational German. It was a huge barrier for her.

Being the determined and ministry-oriented person she is, she refused to allow her lack of German to keep her from serving. She decided she would minister in ways that required a little speaking. She did janitor work at the church and served breakfast to all on Sunday mornings in the living room of the tiny apartment behind the sanctuary, which had formerly served as a parsonage. She entertained church members and first-time visitors at the parsonage for the noon meal. We also hosted a time of fellowship in our apartment after the Sunday evening service. She served coffee, cake, and cookies. This meant baking and freezing these desserts during the week.

Our 5-room complex had two large rooms connected by an 8 ft. high triple-paneled door. This arrangement converted the two rooms into a functional 750 sq.ft. lounge. We would gather there after church and eat, laugh, talk, pray, sing, and plan together.

In the beginning, these Sunday evening gatherings, together with the breakfasts, became one of our Berlin ministry's largest integrating and growth factors. Initially, however, there was not enough money in the church funds to pay for the food. As the congregation's treasury grew, they met the breakfast costs out of church funds. We continued to finance the food for the Sunday evening fellowship out of our small personal budget. However, since it was essential to our ministry, we continued funding it in faith.

About that time, Christa, one of our board members, sensed what was happening. She approached us about supplementing the cost of the Sunday evening food by setting out a decorated and slotted can in the living room for contributions. We told her it was a thoughtful idea, but we refused because we were not seeking repayment. We were doing it out of love for God and our people. Undeterred, she brought us a colorful tin can with a slot on the top. However, we did not feel comfortable putting it out in our living room. We thanked her for her kindness, but explained that we must do this in faith. Christa didn't say anything, but she put the can in the kitchen, on the top corner of our cabinet where it could be reached. Although she told all the church members, we never saw anyone put money in it. It stayed there for seven years.

Our salary did not require a vow of poverty. But neither was our once-a-month check enough to feed all those extra people four times a month without getting tight. We would come to the end of the third week of the month and have nothing left for food. When people asked how we were doing it, I would answer cheerily, "We have a rich Father." It would always be suitable for a chuckle. However, just as the VW bus was the Lord's, so were we, and it reminded us that God would provide.

Several months after Christa had given us the tin can, Mary-Esther, came to me on Friday and asked me for 50 DM for baking goods. I took my wallet out. It was empty. I thanked God for supplying our needs and, in jest, told her to look in the can. She reached for it and took the lid off. As the contents of the can became visible, our eyes became enormous, and our jaws dropped! There was a 50 DM bill in the can.

We rejoiced but disregarded it because we thought Christa must have spotted it and put something in it. I inspected the can several times after that, when finances were not critical, and it was always empty. We both monitored people who would visit and saw no one put anything in it.

However, a few months later, we got into another tight spot. We looked at each other, then at the can. I had checked it out on Sunday night after everyone had left, and it had been empty. I was sure there was nothing in it. We took the tin down and removed the lid. We could not believe our eyes! There, as big as life, was a banknote, again the amount Mary-Esther had asked for. It remains a mystery to this day. When we needed nothing, the tin was empty. But in these and at least a half-dozen subsequent situations, the amount we needed was in that tin can! Whether God or someone put the money in the tin can, the truth remains that God was supplying our needs!

John David's Prayer of Faith

Our apartment house was built in 1898. Much of the wiring and plumbing were still original. One day, our hall lights quit working. I changed the fuse, the starters, and the fluorescent bulbs, but nothing I did could get them to work. John David, who had just turned four, sensed the tension and was just as concerned as his dad. He wanted to know exactly what was wrong and why. We told him as best we could.

And as in most Christian families, we told him we should pray and ask for God's help. After we finished praying, John David exclaimed spontaneously, "I want to pray, too!"

So, we knelt in the hallway, and John David uttered his simple prayer, "Thank you, God, for fixing our lights again. Amen."

After such a prayer of faith, I decided not to call the electrician and asked God to honor John David's prayer. A few weeks went by, and there were still no lights. For a few weeks, I would secretly turn on the switch from time to time, without success.

Then, one day about two months later, Mary-Esther burst into my office, "Tim, Tim, the lights are working!" They had come on by themselves. God had answered the prayer of our four-year-old son.

Lesson Learned

It is unbelievably adventurous, signing everything over to God and making it His property. The important thing was not how the money got in the can but that He supplied exactly what we needed. He will provide for our every need when we need it! The walls we erect, be they monetary, physical, or even intellectual, when torn down by moving out in faith, can be the beginning of Christ's working in and through us. This is true not only individually but also corporately.

The more we invest in the Kingdom of God, under the direction of Christ's Lordship, He always supplies enough to complete the task and still meet our personal needs. Other congregations are making this discovery as well.

No wonder Paul wrote to the Corinthians, *"And God is able to make all grace abound to you, so that in all things at all times, having all you need, you will abound in every good work."* (II Corinthians. 9:8)

CHAPTER 10

LILI IS BORN AT OUR HOUSE

> *"For I was hungry, and you gave me something to eat, I was thirsty, and you gave me something to drink. I was a stranger and you invited me in, I needed clothes, and you clothed me, I was sick, and you looked after me, I was in prison, and you came to visit me." (Matthew 25:35-36)*

Hospitality

The church had some invitation cards the size of business cards printed. They were leaf green with a line-drawing of the church, pertinent information on the front, and a few testimonials on the back.

Our people would take a fistful and pass them out to their friends, colleagues, or anyone they met. It was like one might use a business card to invite them to church. Everyone in the church always had a few cards available on their person. The cards brought people to our church. They would walk up the street on Sunday morning with a card in hand, matching the drawing with the building. The cards seemed to be ubiquitous.

Ruth Schermuly

In June 1976, a young woman named Ruth called us. She was 20 years old and married to a carpenter, Carsten, who was working in West Berlin. She was calling from West Germany. Ruth told us she had an eighteen-month-old son, Christian, in tow and was seven months pregnant with their second child. As her story unfolded, she explained that her marriage was very rocky and that a Christian friend had given her our number. Ruth had called out of desperation and asked that I visit her husband because he had not been returning her calls. I agreed to do so, and she gave me his address.

Curious about how her friend knew our phone number, I asked," How is it you received our number?" The story she related was unbelievable. The Zimmermann family had been in a vacation rental home complex in West Germany. Werner had casually pulled a book out of the bookcase and had read a while. Thinking he might get back to it, he placed the church's green calling card as a bookmark and put it back on the shelf. A friend of Ruth had rented the same house at a later point and had read the same book. The church's bookmark had fallen into her lap. Knowing about Ruth's situation and that her husband, Carsten, was in West Berlin, she gave Ruth the card. It was a perfect example of sowing and reaping.

God has beautiful ways of answering prayer and using what we have given Him. We saw this as God's partial answer to our prayer for more families.

A few days later, on my birthday in 1976, we were on our way to a restaurant to celebrate. Because the restaurant was near Carsten's apartment, I called on him in his one-room flat. The following Sunday, he was in church and became a regular attendee. But I am getting ahead of my story.

Wanting to see his family reunited, Carsten thought he had found an apartment for them. He called Ruth and told her it was all settled and that they could come. On a Wednesday evening in August, she arrived in a taxi at the church. It was the only address she knew. The prayer meeting was just letting out. There she stood, eight months pregnant, with several enormous suitcases, an eighteen-month-old son in tow, and no place to go. I can't imagine a more desperate situation. We had all assumed that Carsten had signed the papers to move into the flat. But he had not. In West Berlin, finding a flat takes month of diligent searching. There was no place for them to go. He had not lied. The landlord had turned him down the day before, discouraging him too much to tell her or us.

What would we do with this family of three, soon to be four? I looked at Mary-Esther, and she nodded. So, we told them they could spend a few nights with us until they found an apartment. We were not yet up to speed on the disastrous, bureaucratized housing market in West Berlin. The days became weeks. Ruth was constantly on the go, looking for a place. Finding an apartment in West Berlin was like looking for an iceberg at the equator.

They had been with us for about four weeks and still had no place to go. One evening we went to bed, and I was sleeping deeply. Suddenly, Mary-Esther, a nurse, was violently shaking me awake. "Get up quickly and get dressed. The baby's coming! I just checked Ruth, and I can see the head! You must take her to the hospital immediately. You do not have a second to waste."

It usually takes me a long time to wake up and get dressed. However, with the ear-splitting screams of a woman in labor, Carsten and I were in our clothes in record time. He told me which hospital they wanted to have the baby delivered. He carried Ruth to the VW bus, laid her on top of Mary-Esther's terry cloth housecoat in the backseat, and we were off. It was 2:30 am and I drove the city streets at 70 mph, with warning lights flashing. Carsten screamed at me in half-hysterical tones, "Hurry, the head is out."

We arrived in less than three minutes and roared up to what we assumed would be the entrance to an emergency room. Just the opposite! It looked like the hospital was closed or empty! The outside window blinds were down. The outside lights were off, and they had rolled down a steel link fence blocking the front door. Ruth was screaming as we frantically looked for a place where we could raise someone but were unsuccessful. We did not need to get out of the bus to see we could not get in through that door. I drove to the corner of the small factory-like brick building to see if anything there might be open. Darkness! At last, I saw what seemed to be a microphone. I got out, pressed the button, and yelled into it several times, "Let us in, a mother is in labor!" No response. In one last act of desperation, Carsten tore the sliding door back and hollered at the top of his lungs, "HILFE! HELP!" many times.

LILI IS BORN AT OUR HOUSE

The hospital was in the middle of a residential section of the city. By this time, lights were on, heads hanging out of windows, watching the drama on the street. Someone was hollering in a language I had to clean up, "Quiet down!" We, however, were still on the outside looking in. Going elsewhere did not come into question.

I drove to the front of the building to make as much noise at the front door as possible. We were frantic! In the middle of a city of two million people, in front of a hospital locked up like Fort Knox, possibly two lives in the balance, and no help in sight. It seemed like hours, yet it was only about three minutes.

As we were pulling around the corner to the front, a nun came running toward us. Ruth was groaning, and we were all shaking like Jell-O inside. The nun said, "I'll explain later; follow me." She led us to the front door, which was now ajar, and they had a stretcher waiting.

They placed Ruth and the baby, almost with us, on the stretcher and began wheeling her down the hall. I parked the van and followed them down the corridor. A midwife had intercepted them halfway down the corridor. When I came within earshot, the nurse said to Ruth, "Press one more time." The midwife was holding the little baby girl upside down in no time, and a nun was tying off the child's umbilical cord.

I looked at my watch. We had lived a lifetime, but only twenty minutes had elapsed since Mary-Esther had roused me from sleep. We were exhausted but grateful. The nuns assured us that both mother and daughter were doing fine.

The nuns then sat us down and explained why the hospital had been closed. The neighbors had complained that the neon lights on the front of the building were too bright and had sued the hospital to have them turned off late at night. The same was true of the blinds, which, when totally closed, were tight enough for an air raid. When they heard us making noise outside, they thought some drunks were fighting, or a man was beating on a woman. But then, gratefully, a midwife had heard Ruth screaming and exclaimed that it was a woman in labor. It was then that the timid nuns were brave enough to come out to see what was taking place.

Our gratitude that everything had gone well was more significant than our exasperation. The Lord had protected us all. Little Elisabeth (Lili) and her mother returned to our place. In a few weeks, the family found an apartment and moved in. Five younger brothers eventually followed Lili. She adopted us as her "aunt and uncle," and she has been a frequent guest in our home.

I said earlier that this family remained in the church. They acknowledged Christ's Lordship and have grown a great deal since then. Carsten was a carpenter by trade, and his gifts in practical ways were a great help in building and renovating. They even named their third child Johannes Timotheus after his "Uncle Tim."

God can use our homes, too, if we allow Him to have them as His domain. This experience enriched all our lives because Werner left the church's card in a book by mistake on vacation. Christ took it from there.

It was not always easy. Having Christ as the Lord of our home life and giving Him control was exhausting. There were times filled with disappointment, frustration, and even feelings of betrayal. But much more, we have felt the excitement and the inner rewards of playing a small part in His Kingdom's work. It was a never-ending adventure.

Lessons Learned

One barrier we erect is the desire to have our own four walls to ourselves. Some people need more privacy than others, but we are all called to do our part. The biblical concept of hospitality includes opening our homes in Christ's love to strangers, the needy, and the hurting.

Every one of Ruth and Carsten's seven children is a Christian today. Christ's Lordship reaches out through His servants in a kind of love that is not easily resisted. And we are all His servants. Who knows? We may host angels, unaware.

CHAPTER 11

GOD'S HEALING POWER

"...intercession is also a daily service we owe to God and our brother. He who denies his neighbor the service of praying for him denies him the service of a Christian. It is clear, furthermore, that intercession is not general and vague but very concrete: a matter of definite people and definite difficulties and therefore of definite petitions. The more definite my intercession becomes, the more promising it is." Dietrich Bonhoeffer, Life Together

The Wall of Timidity

The wall of timidity takes many forms. Witnessing or even being willing to give an answer to those who ask for a reason for our faith, offering believing prayer for healing, and more, are things many Christians shy away from doing. Through the years of our ministry in West Berlin, God did some marvelous things. In times of need and intercession, the church community would gather around the altar for extended periods of corporate prayer.

One way God ministered to us was through our illnesses and His healing. The following are the stories of people touched by God's healing power and whom He used to produce a powerful witness.

Friedrich Behmenburg

Friedrich had begun attending our church just before we arrived. He had a sunny disposition. Everyone loved him, especially the children. He was wise beyond his years and had the gift of being able to correct people so gently and sympathetically that they would often thank him for doing it.

However, he had a rare congenital disease that involved muscle deterioration. There was no cure. This disease then attacked his vital organs and, ultimately, his body's most critical muscle, his heart. Friedrich would tell us how he initially rebelled against the disability, but God had since given him complete peace about it.

It had reached the stage where he had immense difficulty standing from a sitting position. It would take him two or three minutes and several props to accomplish the task. He needed a cane when walking. God's gift to him was a complete personal honesty before God and man. He radiated a warm spirit that could calm edgy nerves and bring peace in a storm. He had become an excellent counselor. His delicate sensitivity to the feelings and needs of people was of great value on the church board.

One of his actual trials was that he felt he would probably never marry. He had been engaged to a fine young woman when we arrived in Berlin and had been thrilled. However, she broke off the engagement, and it took him several weeks to recover.

Not long after that, in the fall of 1974, he began a prayer cell in his apartment and announced it to the others. Three others agreed to meet with him weekly to pray for the congregation, missions, and their personal needs. One person who joined the group was Christa Nitschke, a young single librarian in her mid-twenties. Soon she confessed to the group that she was suffering from loneliness, "But I'll never marry," she was quick to add.

Friedrich began praying that Christa would find a husband, so she would have someone to share her burdens with. Soon, Friedrich, sensitive to the Lord's voice, noticed that God seemed to say to him, "You are the man!"

Straightforward, as the German people are, I valued this trait highly. I never had to wonder what was being said behind my back. Friedrich went to Christa. It was just as she was leaving on vacation. He told her what he felt God was saying to him. "Well, He has NOT spoken to me!" was her quick retort.

Friedrich was unaware that Mary-Esther had been dealing with Christa about bringing her aversion to marriage to God.

Christa had just prayed through on this a few days before Friedrich came to her with his initial proposal.

While she was on vacation, the Lord showed her He was helping her with her loneliness. When she came home, they dated. They do not date casually in Germany. Before a young man asks a young lady out on a date, he usually already has serious intentions. Christa accepted his physical disadvantage; they fell in love and were soon married. It was my first wedding in Germany.

They moved into her second-floor apartment. It was obvious to all that they were good for each other. Christa still had her own difficulties, but they were not as frequent or extreme as before. Friedrich was totally accepting of her and extremely patient.

Only about two years later, his illness had progressed to where he could barely negotiate the stairs. He could walk down, but stepping up would take half an hour. He worked as a tutor at a children's home and had to get down and up daily.

One evening, the exertion must have been too great. Christa called us from the hospital, "they brought Friedrich into the hospital early this morning, and he's doing poorly. It is his heart. Would you come?"

He was up and down for several days. Then he took a turn for the worse. I visited him in the intensive care unit and asked if he would consider being anointed. He said he would. Knowing the sensitivity of the hospital personnel praying over patients, I had asked if three or four men could enter the ICU once to administer a form of "last rights." They agreed.

Dr. V. H. Lewis, one of our denomination's six leaders, was in town for a weekend revival with us. The youth choir from Frankfurt was there to sing. We planned to go to the hospital after the service on Sunday morning.

However, around 6:00 am Christa called. "Tim, if you want to see 'Behmie' (pronounced Bay-mee) alive, you must come now. The doctor has told me he will not last more than a few hours. His heart muscle has atrophied, and he is going fast."

I called Werner and Dr. Lewis and asked them if they would accompany me immediately. They both agreed. Werner met me at the house, and we went to pick up Dr. Lewis at the Pension. On the way to the hospital, we brought Dr. Lewis up to date on Friedrich and why our visit was so urgent. He had a pastor's heart.

After talking briefly with Friedrich about his relationship with Christ and the certainty of God's promises, each of us prayed the prayer of faith that God would heal Friedrich.

After the worship service, lunch, and a short time of fellowship with Dr. Lewis, I drove him to the airport. There was a special bond between us, since he had been the person who had ordained us in 1971. I thanked him for his understanding and for coming to minister to us. I was extremely grateful. We said goodbye, and he flew to his next appointment.

That evening in church, the news on Friedrich was not encouraging. He was worse.

Someone said, "all our prayers were for nothing!" I could not let that stand. I replied, "That is not how we should be thinking. He is still alive, and until he takes his last breath, I, for one, will believe God can still heal him."

Two weeks later, Friedrich came home from the hospital. The doctors could not explain his complete recovery. Even his heart seemed strong. We were rejoicing because, according to the doctors, he should have already been in his grave. He and Christa installed a stair lift to their first-floor apartment so he could come and go.

Five years later, after God miraculously had healed Friedrich, He exercised that love that is greater and broader than we can comprehend. He took Friedrich, age 49, to be with Himself forever. There, he has no more struggles to stand, no more cane, no more wheelchair, and no more gasping for breath. Thank you, Jesus, for his life of complete surrender to Your Lordship.

Christian Hilliges

Christian, a pastor's son, had gone to the university to study pharmacy. He was a leader in the Young Communists while there. After being a Transcendental Meditation instructor for three years. When he came to our church, he had been a Christian for about three years. He had surrendered his life to Christ and was growing in the faith.

One day, he went to the doctor for the results of a test. The doctor sat down on the corner of his desk, looked somberly at Christian, and said, "I am sorry to tell you this. We are going to have to admit you to the hospital immediately. I have found a growth that is likely to be malignant. We will take a biopsy and wait until we have the lab work back."

With these life-shattering words, Christian left the doctor's office, went home, and explained the news to his wife and three children. When he called me, I drove over immediately to spend time with them. I asked Christian how all of this was affecting him. He answered without hesitation, "I feel God's peace. I am confident that God has a purpose in all of this, and He wants to glorify Himself through it."

As soon as a bed was available, they admitted Christian to a room with two other men. One was a young Turkish man, and the other was a slightly older German patient. As was typical of Christian, he began witnessing to his two roommates. The German man turned away toward the window whenever Christian talked about Christ. The young man from Turkey seemed amazingly open. This was unusual because even in Germany, the Turkish people are very loyal to Islam. Christian spoke to him about God's peace amid life's storms and how Christ was taking away his fear in the face of cancer. The German roommate showed no interest.

The operation went well. The mass was gone, and the biopsy came back negative.

We were all rejoicing, but Christian took it in stride. A few days later, while Christian was having his quiet time, the Lord laid it on his heart to go visit his uninterested roommate.

To his great surprise, the young man who had previously seemed entirely uninterested greeted Christian cheerily. After a brief conversation that turned into one about the Lord, he prayed the sinner's prayer and accepted Christ as his personal Savior. Ten days later, Christian returned to revisit him, only to learn that he had passed away a few days earlier. As we talked later, Christian said,

> "I cannot shake the feeling that God allowed that growth in my body to place me next to that young man so he could accept Christ. I am convinced that through my sickness God was answering the fervent prayer of some believing relative or friend for his salvation. It was worth going through the entire ordeal for him to find God. I never expected to have an answer to my prayer so soon. He certainly glorified Himself through my illness."

Klaus Dykoff

Klaus was typical of many on the drug scene in Berlin. He left home early, and his first contact with drugs was in his hometown, a rural part of West Germany. He started using drugs because he was bored and disillusioned with life.

In his wanderings, he arrived in West Berlin and found a job, but as is often the case, he again gravitated towards friends who were part of "the drug scene." He began taking pills and then graduated to hard drugs of all kinds. For about two years, he became increasingly entangled in the emotional and physical degeneration that goes along with drug abuse: lack of initiative, poor eating habits, depressing conversation, and speaking unconnected sentences.

One day, he forgot to turn off the water. It overflowed his bathroom tub, dripping into the apartment below. Annemarie, a young career woman living there, was a Christian who attended our church. While helping her clean up the mess, he noticed a religious poster on the wall and asked if she was a Christian, which she confirmed. The poster had awakened childhood memories in Klaus about Children's Church. Immediately, he was under conviction. In a childlike way, he asked her if she could help him find God. Annemarie led him to Christ that afternoon and brought him to church the following Sunday.

Klaus has a powerful testimony wherever he goes. He had held a responsible job in a growing firm but chose to further his education at a local university.

At one point, he worked three and a half days per week to spend the rest of his time in the Lord's work. He worked in Caravan (like Scouts), helping to fill the void left by Thomas and Esther because they had gone to pastor our second church. The children loved him.

He has a gift for street evangelism. In the summer of 1983, I led a seven-week open-air evangelism project in Kassel. Klaus joined us in Kassel for the last two weeks. It was a joy to see how fearlessly he preached and how effectively he talked with people one-on-one.

He could talk with authority and experience how God can take away the appetites that destroy and replace them with new desires that bring new life.

One day, a young man approached me on the street in Kassel's main square. He was excited about the paranormal and everything they could do, from bending spoons to lifting tables off the floor. Then he challenged me to lift the table off the ground, and he would believe in Jesus. I asked him, "Why would I want God to do something I can do myself?

I called Klaus over and introduced them. I explained the gist of our conversation to Klaus and asked him, "Can you tell us briefly what your life was like in the drug scene and whether you could kick it on your own?" Klaus faced the young man and explained how hopelessly addicted he had been. Then I asked Klaus, "How did you get from there to here?" Klaus told the young man how Christ had changed his life instantly and how he could now serve Him with joy and abandon.

I turned to the young man and asked, "In your sessions, are people freed and given joy like Klaus has received?" He did not answer. "The power of God we are proclaiming changes lives. Bending spoons and levitating tables are child's play for God. Would you like to have us pray with you to receive the God of the truly miraculous?" He shook his head and walked away.

Lessons Learned

Where Christ is truly Lord of His Church, He will be Lord in every area of our beings. We are not just spiritual beings. We still have emotions, wills, and bodies that may need healing. Christ's Lordship extends into every area of our lives. Klaus and Annemarie did not go out and witness in a structured way. They simply talked about Christ and what he meant to their lives all the time.

If we can ask for more grace to break down the barriers of our timidity and our "little faith," He will do much more than we can imagine. He desires that all His children use the gifts He gives us. He wants us to exercise our spiritual faith muscles in everyday situations so naturally that He can work within His Church to bring His healing, strength, faith, justice, and all the Fruit of the Spirit to everyone we meet. And He is glorified!

CHAPTER 12

WONDERFULLY MULTICULTURAL

Christ opened up the way to God and to our brother. Now Christians can live with one another in peace, love, and serve one another; they can become one. But they can continue to do so only by way of Jesus Christ. Only in Jesus Christ are we one. Only through him are we bound together. To eternity he remains the one Mediator." Dietrich Bonhoeffer, Life Together

A Wall That Resists Welcoming People of Color

Most evangelical churches, except for possibly a few people of color in attendance, are homogeneously White. As the community changes, the church population should change accordingly. Evangelicals are more fellowship oriented. When the community changes and different people move in, the tendency is for the church people to move first. Then the people who remain with the church drive in. That is an oversimplification, and there are many exceptions.

West Berlin, a city of two million people, was also remarkably culturally diverse. People from over 100 nations were represented in the population in this city of over two million. People arrived at the doors of our church from all over the world. Students from Indonesia, El Salvador, Ghana, India, England, and the United States worshipped at our church.

A very gratifying affiliation with Campus Crusade for Christ, known in Germany as "Campus," brought many new Christian students from other countries into our congregation. They all soon became vital contributing members of our Christian community. When the time came for them to return home, they would go firmly grounded in their faith, ready to contribute to the church's growth in their home countries.

The second group of people who attended included those employed in West Berlin, either by the occupying forces, the economy, or were looking for political asylum in West Berlin. They came from the U.S., India, Ghana, France, and England. The rest of the people were our longer-term guests in our apartment.

No matter where they were from, their acceptance into the congregation was almost seamless. The immigrants enriched the community's quest to commit to the Lordship of Christ. Here are a few of their stories.

Gloria and Carlos Gutierrez – El Salvador

Gloria and Carlos were students from El Salvador. Gloria had many challenging health issues, which God helped her overcome against all odds. The church prayed faithfully for Gloria during the two times she hovered near death. But her healing was miraculous, and we all praised God for this gifted couple.

After she recovered and could attend, they would come on Sunday evenings. He was a talented classical guitarist and would play during the fellowship time after the service in our apartment. Imagine low lights, candles, people in all kinds of quiet conversation, the smell of German coffee, with the warm tones of guitar music as background. Christian Fellowship of richness, with people from around the world, was inspiring and unforgettable.

Our seven-year-old son, John, was taking classical guitar lessons. Carlos was an excellent teacher. They played simple but beautiful duets during the afterglow when Carlos was there. Another example of passing on the gifts God has given us.

After they had earned their degrees, they moved back to their beloved El Salvador. They had talked often and earnestly about the plight of their people and were returning to make a difference.

Slamet, Matilde, and Tobias Basuki – Indonesia

Slamet Basuki was a student at the Technical University. While there, he completed his doctorate in mathematics. He and his wife

Matilda also had a young son named Tobias. They moved back to Indonesia, where he has had a successful career as an educator and researcher. Through the years, they established a track record of embracing their Muslim neighbors as they would treat Christ. We all remember when there was a wave of violence against Christians in that country. The vigilantes wanted to harm their homes and family, but their Muslim neighbors protected them. Their son, born in West Berlin, is now a respected broadcaster in Jakarta.

Gisela Abraham – India

Gisela Abraham had been married to a successful Indian business executive. After their divorce, she moved back to her hometown with her three German Indian children, Anita, Ramona, and her younger son, Danny, who was about John's age.

All four of them became active in the church. John and Danny became fast friends at church. Anita, then a mature eleven-year-old, taught the Toddler's class, and Gisela taught the older children.

Five Politicians in Exile – Ghana

Five exiled Christian politicians from Ghana had officially sought political asylum, which the German government granted. Timothy and several of his friends began attending the church in March 1980. Prison or execution was their fate had they stayed in their home country. Hans Joachim Hahn, one leader from "Campus," provided simultaneous translation during the morning sermon in the back corner of the room. We held weekly Bible Studies in the asylum housing on Thursday evenings.

They asked me a question that has haunted me to this day. "Pastor, we became Christians because of the wonderful Christian missionaries from Germany. We thought all Germans were Christians like that. Why have we not found anyone on the street who knows about Jesus?" Such beautiful, simple faith!

I noticed they seemed to sing English hymns dutifully and with little affect. So, I asked them if they could teach us some songs they sang back home. There was a pause. Then the young man who seemed in charge smiled broadly, excused himself, and brought back a guitar and several additional young men I had not yet met. They introduced themselves and discussed briefly what they wanted to sing first. When they began, the room came alive with their joy, harmonies, rhythms, movement, and simple but powerful Christian lyrics. They ministered to us.

I invited them to teach an Advent song about Mary to the congregation. They sang in delightfully African-accented English, and it was a big hit. Their music added to the reality that we celebrated Advent worldwide even as we were singing.

When we were renovating the villa, they also came to help. They wallpapered side by side with the rest of the congregation.

Some Stayed Briefly in our Apartment.

When Thomas and Esther arrived, the renovation in Grunewald was just beginning. They were with us for a few days before we negotiated a weekly cost for them to stay at a nearby pension.

As I mentioned earlier in Chapter one, Peter (Phineas), this was the time a young gay Jewish man, took sanctuary in our home to avoid sexual exploitation. Several of his friends also attended the church services regularly.

Heidi Mueller, a recent college graduate and singer/songwriter came to stay with us for a few months as a jumping-off point to visit relatives in the German Democratic Republic (DDR). We cleared a Sunday evening service for her to give us a concert. Since then, she has experienced success as a performing artist.

Anne Raudsepp, a family friend, came to live with us for six months while studying German at Goethe Institute. She had helped my parents with housekeeping while my grandparents lived with them. When she was with us, the Schermuly family came to stay with us. Her help with all our guests was incalculable.

Lessons Learned

Besides those mentioned above, people from India, France, England, the United States, and the U. S. Forces were also present in the congregation on most Sunday mornings. There was no adverse reaction to the multicultural make-up of our church that reached my ears. The rhythm of the community remained steady, each person ministering to the others according to their gifts. The overarching theme of the church was that we were on the journey to Christlikeness together. Our complexion or country of origin paled to insignificance in the light of our highest goal, "To be like Jesus." And we really needed each other to finish well.

CHAPTER 13

VENGEANCE IS MINE SAYS THE LORD

"For if you forgive others their trespasses, your heavenly Father will also forgive you; 15 but if you do not forgive others, neither will your Father forgive your trespasses." (Matthew 6:14-15, NRSV)

The Wall of Unforgiveness

Perhaps the most consequential and nearly unconquerable wall that holds back the Holy Spirit's working in our lives and the congregation's life is that of unforgiveness.

Herr Müller (not his name) began attending our church in the spring of 1977. He was initially very enthusiastic about our church and wanted to join immediately. However, I had a standing rule not to take anyone into membership until they had been a regular attender for at least six months, giving us time to assess their Christian walk.

However, he had become overly critical of a larger Pentecostal church and began writing what he called, "information letters", which he claimed were exposing them as counterfeit Christians. He approached me quietly about putting these "hate letters" on our free literature table.

Another principle I have long followed is never to speak ill of other Christian groups nor let it knowingly take place in my church. It did not matter who it was, or whether I agreed with the group in question. So, I politely but firmly explained my position to Herr Müller and said no. He seemed to take it well.

However, from then on, a wall grew between us that kept growing. Within just a few weeks, Herr Müller's excitement had given way to moodiness and suspicion. He asserted that we were out to ruin his plan to uncover the "heresy" of the other church and destroy it.

Some parishioners dreaded his arrival because he would even interrupt the sermon from time to time to ask unsnswerable questions. He planned to trap the answerer. He criticized our hymnal (we did not yet have our own) with the words, "You have the same dirty songs about the Holy Spirit in your hymnal they have in theirs."

Our attempts to love and draw him into fellowship seemed to fall on deaf ears. By this point, I became increasingly disturbed about his spiritual and emotional state.

The board wanted me to forbid him access to the services, but I believed love and acceptance could win. I asked them to give him more time. However, the further I tried to help him, the more vehement he became. Twice, when he rose to hit me in a larger circle for Bible Study, the men had to restrain him.

I had already talked with him without a result. The board approached him according to Matthew 18. Two male board members accompanied me to his apartment to talk. We were no longer assured he would not become violent. With witnesses, he did not become violent. He still felt he was in the right, and in his mind, everything to do with the Holy Spirit needed to be eliminated.

I discovered he had relatives in West Berlin and found out if he was having trouble with them. The conversation with his uncle was revealing. The family had come from East Germany, and his mother had raised him according to the philosophy that love was the key. Love, for her, meant to be non-authoritarian. He abused his mother to the point where she was forced to flee to an unknown location in West Germany. He had spent some time in the secret police prison in East Berlin, and he had not been the same since.

Several days later, Mary-Esther and John flew to the United States on an early August morning, at 5:00 am, to visit her parents. I was to follow a week later. Thomas and Esther had completed their practicum (internship) and had left that morning to return to Switzerland and the Bible College. I was alone in the apartment and had gone back to bed.

At 10:00 am, the telephone roused me. Herr Müller was on the other end, and he was seething. "You were with my uncle and talked with him about everything I have done!" I had not been with his uncle, and we had not talked about everything.

I recognized East German secret police interrogation techniques. I was supposed to reply, "Oh no, not that way, it was this way." Using these methods, he could usually get all the information he wanted and then use it to terrorize others. His accusation was not totally false, as I have already described, but far too extreme. In addition, I had his family, my family, and the congregation to protect.

So, I had long since determined he would not get any information out of me using this trick; I had never fallen prey to his tactics. For this, I was on his blacklist.

Fighting sleep, I was determined not to implicate his uncle or cause more trouble for him. I also did not want to lie. So, instead, I answered, "Herr Müller, your information is inaccurate." He repeated his accusation, and I repeated my answer. Then, abruptly, he hung up on me.

I got up, ate a quick breakfast, and went to my home office for my quiet time. About 10:30 am, I had a strange but strong feeling about taking the letter I had written the evening before to the mailbox. At first, I thought it was the enemy with his usual distractions. But it got stronger. Suddenly, on impulse, I got up and left the house for the mailbox across the intersection and through a short walkway to a more traveled corner. I deposited the letter, and on the way back, just as I came to a spot beside an advertising column.

Out of the corner of my eye, coming from the right, I saw Herr Müller charging toward the corner on the other side of the wide street looking very angry. Putting two and two together, I knew where he was headed and I did not want to be alone with him. I stopped and slipped out of sight behind the advertising column while he went straight into our house. Not feeling it would be wise to continue, I remained where I was. He then went to the church and looked in the office window to see if I was there, then he left. I was sure God had prompted the urge to mail the letter.

Just before noon, the congregation's Christian Life Director, Eberhard Wunderlich, arrived to finish preparations for the Sunday school during my vacation absence. He had not been there ten minutes when the doorbell rang. I went to the door. It was Herr Müller again. With a livid face, he repeated his earlier accusation.

I tried to bar his entrance into the apartment with my foot behind the door. In a flash, his fist came through the crack in the door and hit my face with such force that I could not maintain my balance. He stormed into the hallway, swinging his fists, hitting me repeatedly, and spewing epithets.

It surprised me it was not hurting. I peddled back to the living room hoping Eberhard would witness this. Herr Müller had picked this time because he thought there would be no witnesses. My nose was bleeding intensely. I ducked into the kitchen so it would not stain the rug in the hallway. I thought, "I'm so glad Mary-Esther and John David are not here."

By then, Eberhard said he could see what was happening. Herr Müller suddenly realized that there was a witness in the apartment. The moment I slipped into the kitchen, he strode back down the corridor, slammed the front door, and disappeared as quickly as he had come.

Eberhard took a few polaroids of my face, and the floor in case we needed any proof in court. We then cleaned up my face and the blood on the floor.

That incident convinced us both that Herr Müller had crossed the line and needed to be stopped. We sat down, finished our planning session, and then went to the police station to file charges.

My analysis was that his mother had never given him any boundaries. He would test them to see how far he could go. When he found none, he would become increasingly demanding until he felt free to terrorize and use force to get his way. I was convinced that putting a wall of legal protection around my congregation and my family was necessary.

When we finished at the police station, the excitement was more than I had thought. I was still shaking with mild shock. I was starting supper when the doorbell rang. It was Thomas and Esther. They had been turned back at the border (80 miles away) because he was driving a car registered in Germany with a Swiss driver's license. They grimaced at my face and inquired, "Whatever happened to you? Did you run into a door?" I explained the day's events to them and told them I was delighted to see them because I was not sure what Herr Müller would do next. I invited them to join me, and we sat down to eat supper.

We had barely taken the first bite when the doorbell rang. It was Herr Müller. We did not open the door, and he pounded on the door with his fists and feet. One of the door's lower solid oak panels shattered, leaving a head-sized hole in the door. He got down on his hands and knees and put his head through the hole, screaming at the top of his lungs about how we were dirty pigs and how he would destroy us. His mouth was foaming; he had really worked himself up.

I called the police immediately and reported that the same man I had reported earlier, had returned and damaged the property. They came, recorded the damage, and left.

Again, in Thomas and Esther, God had sent witnesses and comfort on the day I was supposed to have been alone. With all the violence, I was unsure whether it was safe to stay in the apartment alone during the week before flying to the USA.

I called the church board together and explained the situation to them. They were unanimously in favor of barring him legally from setting foot on our apartment or the church property. We contacted a lawyer who drew up an appropriate restraining order.

Father Forgive Him

I had already forgiven Herr Müller for what he had done. My problem was the guilt I felt for not being able to help him more.

Once he had his boundary, he did not cross it. He would return to the sidewalk bordering the church property, stop and look in. Still, he heeded his lawyer's advice and did not disobey the Hausverbot or the restraining order barring him from setting foot on the premises. However, we were determined to follow through with the court proceedings to finalize the boundary we had, regretfully, set for him.

After the hearing, the judge's decision was that he was to pay half of the door repair, pay a 500 DM fine to charity, and do 100 hours of community service. He never paid for the door. I avoided him because I had had enough of his kind of exchange. He had threatened to do me bodily harm if he ever met me on the street. It was not easy, because he lived around the corner. I could only pray for him. He was giving the same grief to at least one other pastor in the city and knew he was walking on thin ice.

Every time I saw him, he seemed angrier and more disturbed.

In 1982, not long after we moved to Frankfurt, I received a phone call from Werner. We exchanged pleasantries, and then he turned to the reason for his call. "Did you hear about Herr Müller?" "No," I replied.

"They found him in his apartment a week ago. He had hung himself. They did not discover his body until several weeks after he did it."

"Oh God," I prayed, "Forgive me for not doing more for him." The question still plagues me, "Did we do our best?"

Lessons Learned

As I look back, despite this challenging time, the church grew numerically and spiritually, personally, and collectively. It welded us closer than ever before. It did not discourage us. We were more convinced than ever that we must be in the will of God, or the enemy would not have been resisting so strongly. We knew we were observing tiny fissures in the "gates of hell." Our most significant task was to ensure that Christ remained Lord outside of necessary legal restraints and that we allow Him to fight for us.

It is unimportant the threat or from which direction the attack comes. Within the Lordship of Christ, there is a refuge, strength, and growth to be found in Him. The battle begins when God works in Satan's dark domain. Those experiences were a reality for us. Is it not interesting that Herr Müller's quest was to quell the teaching of the Holy Spirit? Who could ever accomplish that?

Charles Swindoll once said that the most significant opportunities come ingeniously disguised as unsolvable problems. This is an accurate statement, particularly for those who are ministering within the total Lordship of Christ. This is true because we have partnered with the living and almighty God of the universe.

The wall of an unforgiving spirit must come down before He can work. The Lordship of Christ extends through our prayer for forgiveness, reaches infinitely beyond our persons, and breaks through the barriers that men and the enemy can erect. If we link up with the Almighty, there is nothing that can stop His plan from succeeding.

PART III
THE STRUGGLE OF CHRIST'S LORDSHIP

CHAPTER 14

LORD, WE CANNOT AFFORD IT

"Jesus looked at them and said, "With man, this is impossible, but with God, all things are possible." (Matt. 19:26)

Too Little Faith

By 1976, our Sunday school had outgrown its facilities. We had to stagger classes to get everyone in. Even the bedrooms in our apartment were being used. The plan was to build a small addition on the back of our small prefab church building to ease the pressure on our Sunday school and our apartment.

It would be a multi-purpose room with accordion dividers, creating eight Sunday school classrooms. We could also open it into making one large room for breakfasts and other fellowship. But the city refused us a building permit because we would have had to build it too close to the back line of the property.

Since they had placed our existing building farther back on our property, we thought about trying to expand on the front of the building. We got bids on how much it might cost and found out it would cost at least 220,000 DM (or $100,000). We had known that even in 1976, it would not be cheap. The price was not out of line, but the amount jolted us.

On the one hand, we believed God was in it. There was no way our church would raise that kind of money. We had just stretched our budget to become self-supporting.

The Prayer Meeting

We decided to ask Him for His plan to pay for the addition. He would have to give us directions. We called the board together

LORD, WE CANNOT AFFORD IT

for an evening of Stillezeit centered on the question, "Lord, how are we ever going to raise $100,000?" It might as well have been a million.

We were all seated in our living room in a circle. I gave a short devotional, and then we moved into an extended time of quiet prayer and reflection. Each member was to pray and listen to God, asking Him for wisdom and guidance. We wrote those things that came to our minds as we sought His presence. It did not matter what it was.

After 30 minutes of silence and prayer, I asked that we share what the Lord had said to us around the circle. Each one spoke without interruption. Then Christian Hilliges, who was not typically very vocal, expressed that the Lord had directed him to the story of the "Feeding of the Five Thousand." As he had read it, the Lord had seemed to say to him, "This young man brought what he had to Jesus, even though it was not nearly enough to do the job. If you bring all you have, I will take care of the rest."

Everyone was taking notes while each spoke, asking questions or commenting later. After everyone had shared, and all questions asked and answered, we took ten more minutes of quiet time to verify if anything we had shared was from God.

About halfway around the circle, the second time, we realized that the comments were the same. I polled them, and we discovered it was unanimous. We believed God had just given us the "Feeding of the Five Thousand" as our promise. He told us, "Give me your five loaves and two fish, and I'll supply the rest."

At the point of making this discovery, we were all silent for at least a minute. Then a single nun said softly, "During the second quiet time, the Lord spoke to me and said that my five loaves and two fish are to give my next year's salary ($16,000). Because I live and eat at work, I will only keep a little pocket change."

We were all stunned! Then someone else divulged a similar conversation with God and pledged to sell his camper worth about $3,200. A third person said he would sell the heirloom gold watch and heavy gold chain he had inherited from his father. A fourth said, "I don't have any money, but I can make attractive handcrafts. I will make them at my cost, sell them, and give the proceeds to the building fund." Those were holy moments.

It all happened so quickly! We all sat there, stunned. I closed my tear-blurred eyes and wondered, was it like this in Jerusalem when people sold what they had to meet the church's needs? Their spontaneous faith and the unity we felt in those moments was a spiritual experience none of us will ever forget. My only prayer was, "Lord, reward their uncompromising faith by keeping Your promise." At that moment, we were confident that God could remove mountains; nothing was too big for Him. But God would test the strength of our faith again.

When I reflect on Christian, through whom God had spoken, I am reminded of the miracle of his conversion. He was the son of a State Church pastor but had tried many other things to find happiness.

Then, he met Hans Joachim Hahn on the university campus and accepted Christ. Now a pharmacist, he had become a pillar in our congregation, a local preacher, and someone I mentored. I asked him to describe what the Lordship of Christ means to him. The following is His Christian testimony.

Christian Hilliges

"The first two years of my Christian life went by with no significant problems. Then the question of why I was a Christian troubled me. The only answer I had at first was that it was right. As the problem persisted, I realized pride had found its way into my life. But I ignored it. I knew pride was destroying my love for Christ, but it took a while before I was willing to confess it and give it to Him.

"To submit to the Lordship of Christ in my life meant to confess and completely surrender my pride to Him and pursue loving Christ with all my heart, soul, mind, and strength. Two things gave me guidance and assurance of His presence. The first is a Bible verse.

"I will give you a new heart and put a new spirit in you; I will remove from you your heart of stone and give you a heart of flesh. And I will put my Spirit in you and move you to follow my decrees and be careful to keep my laws." (Ezekiel 36:26-27)

"The second thing was the counsel given to John Wesley before he had an assurance of salvation. He was told to preach it until he had it and then to preach it because he had it. I began to pray for and live this life of love for Christ until I received Him, and now I can testify that through His Spirit, I can live it because I have Him."

We now had a metaphor around which we could describe the effort. We planned a meeting for the following Sunday to encourage the rest of the congregation to give to the building project. I prepared a large placard for the occasion. With rudimentary tools and amateur skill, I fashioned two outstretched Styrofoam hands with five loaves and two fish. I glued the 3-D sculpture onto a poster board thermometer with the current giving and placed it in a prominent place.

After the message, I told the story of our board meeting and the campaign's theme and presented the chart. Several board members also testified to the events of the meeting.

In response, a member not on the board, who had suffered a recent stroke, gave the insurance settlement for a specially outfitted car. When the service was over, the small congregation had provided over 80,000 DM in pledges toward the 220,000 DM goal.

This was, of course, not the end of our search for funds. The congregation continued to find new ways to raise money. For example, we all cleaned out our closets and cupboards of things we were not using and sold them at the big flea market downtown. This also provided an outlet for Christa's handcrafts. From donated items people no longer wanted, we raised over 11,000 DM on a huge flea market over the next six months.

Lesson Learned

God had given us a glimpse of His ability to supply our needs according to our faith. We experienced His power when ministering together in unity. After God had whispered the solution to me in my Stillezeit, He had brought us to a consensus and this kind of outcome. It was way beyond my ability to understand. but my trust in His guidance had grown immensely.

CHAPTER 15

THE GATES OF HELL CANNOT RESIST HIS VICTORY

"You are the God who performs miracles; you display your power among the peoples." (Psalm 77:14)

The Walls of Opposition

Can you remember any time you undertook something bigger than yourself that obstacles seemed to arise out of nowhere in the attempt to thwart it? If so, I'm sure you discovered that nothing could stand in the way of ultimate victory. I believe that is one aspect of what Jesus meant when He said, "And the gates of hell will not prevail against it."

When we experience walls, we have found that God has a more suitable solution. Well, we encountered it several more times. The city-planning office rejected the plan we had submitted that would cost 220,00 DM or $100,000.

Well, we experienced impatience, an additional boundary. Jesus often called it "little faith." We are often prone to stop believing because of delays or events that seem to cause the death of the dream.

However, in the end, the "gates of hell" will be breached, and we realize that our initial undertakings would have fallen far short had we not allowed Him to bring His plans into play.

A New Direction

Soon after, Richard Zanner came to West Berlin to meet with the church board and discuss our alternatives. After taking a closer look at our plans, he told us the sanctuary and our planned annex were too small for our expected growth. In his opinion, a new building was needed to meet our growth needs. We explained to him that our financial limits were already exceeded. He replied that he understood, but if we decided to build new and raise as much as possible, he would work on his end to help get some more.

On the strength of his recommendation, we invited several architects to enter a competition for conceptual plans and drawings. The winner was Herr Löwe, who presented a fascinating and spacious building that used every allowable square inch of our land according to code. He drew up plans and submitted them to the city, and they issued a "pre-permit," in principle, pending the approval of the structural details.

Somehow, one of the neighbors found out about the pre-permit and asked if he and the rest of the neighbors could see the plans. They came over to our apartment, looked at the graphs, and asked a few questions, which we answered openly. After they left, their demeanor did not leave us with a good feeling.

A few days after the viewing, one of the neighbors, an excellent lawyer, came over to our place and told us he was sorry to do it, but the seven neighbors had decided to sue the city and its decision to allow us to build. No offense was intended, but they felt they had to protect their interests. The effect of their suit meant we could not proceed with our plans until a court decision.

I asked them, "Why are you doing this?" Their answers varied. One of them said that she liked things the way they were. A second person replied that, given our present growth rate, an increase in people would not be far behind. That might encourage the opening of a kindergarten, creating weekday noise. A third neighbor explained that a high building would rob them of their morning sun. The family in the condo behind our property was afraid the terrace planned for the second floor would disturb his backyard privacy.

The neighbors' lawsuit precipitated a court battle that lasted almost two years. At this point, I remarked to Mary-Esther, "If they succeed in forcing us to go elsewhere to build, I am afraid someone else will move in, and be more difficult to live with than we would have ever been." We prayed that our relationship would remain cordial, no matter the outcome.

God Provides Yet another Way

After the lawsuit was filed, Rev. Zanner called us and suggested that we should begin looking for another lot on which to build. My answer was, "God is in this; He will not let us down!" About two weeks later, he called again, "Tim, it's still bothering me. I really feel we need to begin looking for other property." His second call grabbed my attention.

Were the neighbors to win, we would either need to: a) make such concessions that would make it not advisable to build on that property, or b) begin with our planning starting at go. Were we to win, we would have to contend with disgruntled neighbors who could make our existence equally problematic. All things considered, the lawsuit itself provided enough reason for us to begin looking. It was a bitter pill to swallow.

Based on our previous experience, we decided that if it were God's will to leave, He would certainly have something better for us. This also became the hope of our church people.

By the third time we talked in December, I agreed to begin what turned out to be a six-month search for a new property. It proved a more difficult task than I could ever have imagined.

Initially, I went to city hall to look for vacant lots near us on the city maps. There were some beautiful lots on or near the main arteries in our area. The lot needed to be twice as large as our present one and not have any old-growth trees that the city ordinance required to remain standing. Then, I searched for the owners' addresses and wrote them query letters to ask if they would be willing to talk about selling their property. We discovered that virtually all the owners were living either in East or West Germany and all were unwilling to sell. It seemed impossible to find unimproved lots within two miles of our current location in the "Walled City." After going through this exercise 30-40 times without a glimmer of interest, we exhausted possible building lots near our present location. Those who owned any land in West Berlin considered it an investment in the city's future and better than money in the bank.

Finally, just before our vacation in June, I called our architect, Herr Löwe, and asked him what else we might do. He told me he had also been thinking and wondered if the city might be interested in trading our property with something the city had in their inventory. He agreed to accompany me to City Hall.

On the day before we left on vacation, Herr Löwe and I went to the office of Herr Deichert, the Borough Property Manager. We told him of our plight and asked if the city would be agreeable to the possibility of swapping properties. He replied that he was aware of our situation. At first, I was taken aback but then reminded myself that he must have been involved in our story from the beginning. "Well," he said with a slight smile, "I have two properties which would come into question for you. One is a former police station on Bismarckallee, a well-traveled street, and the other is on a side street nearby. Both are vacant." He showed us the locations on his map. He then picked up the phone and called the person in charge of the Youth Department, who showed immediate interest in a swap. They were looking for childcare property in our neighborhood, and our building would be a perfect solution.

Herr Deichert then suggested that we inspect each property and choose one. Then he would initiate the necessary legal formalities. For the first time, we had hope. If the neighbors won the lawsuit, we now had a possible alternative. We left for our vacation relieved and able to relax.

Both processes continued side-by-side: the suit on the one hand and the swap on the other. Our day in court came, and we all went to testify. The neighbors had prepared their case carefully, and the most influential of them testified. I also read a prepared statement. My impression was that the city lawyers were going through the motions. They had no stake in the outcome.

The Neighbors Won

The legal process was over, and the neighbors won. The possibility of building on the Reichenhallerstrasse property was history. By that time, however, the negotiations for the swap were almost far enough to sign the papers. The Lord had been good to us. Our only cost was to purchase the square meter difference between the size of the two properties. The new building was a massive brick-and-mortar, three-story villa built in AD 1898. It had most recently served as a police station.[9] God had given us a much larger building for a fraction of the cost of new construction. The buildings were an even swap. Of course, there were massive renovations, and we obligated ourselves to restore the provisional roof to its historical dimensions.

Then we heard that the city had decided to open a kindergarten in Reichenhallerstrasse. We were shocked. Mary-Esther immediately reminded me of what I had said at the beginning of the lawsuit. Our poor neighbors must come to terms with a city daycare center.

The Incredible Progression

The modest plans for a small annex had grown through several stages. Beyond our goals, the need for space was growing. We were on the threshold of a building project far beyond our wildest imaginations. The swapped property was a large villa less than three miles from the Gedächtnisskirche at center of West Berlin. It was located at the residential head of the world-famous Kurfürstendamm, and one block from a freeway exit. God had indeed provided something better!

When we returned to visit a year later, the "Green Party," whose pedagogical methods were environmental and non-authoritarian, had moved in. The front yard was fenced along the sidewalk, the lawn had been allowed to grow wild, and an old VW Bug was stripped and buried up to its axles in the gravel parking lot. They had built a pyramid of old tires and a soccer wall for target practice against the front of the building. I am certain the children loved it.

Our former neighbors had inherited a new normal. We are praying that they will be able to enjoy their evenings and weekends.

Some Seed Will Produce a Hundred-Fold

The congregation was founded in 1961 by Pastor Bröhl and his wife, Sonia. Then, in 1963, the Lord laid it on the heart of a generous Texas businessman, Elmer Trimble, to give $10,000 to purchase property on Reichenhallerstrasse in West Berlin. Home Missions put the modest prefabricated building on it. As the years passed, the political situation stabilized considerably. Property values went up.

The value of the land itself was the only part of the swap to be figured into the transaction. The buildings were valued at zero.

The building on Bismarckallee was at least four times larger and cost nothing. It had originally been a villa, built by an army colonel in 1898 before WWI, but it had been through the war and renovation. After our renovation was completed, it included:

- A beautiful 150-person sanctuary with a decorative wood ceiling
- A one-bedroom apartment on the first floor, with a bath and kitchen
- Another large two-story apartment in the spacious attic under the new roof,
- A spacious youth room,
- Two brand new bathrooms in the basement,
- Sunday school classrooms on the second floor,
- A pastor's study, and
- A new electrical and heating system.

Soon after it was finished, it was valued at over $2,000,000. The gift of Elmer Trimble in 1963 had increased 2,000-fold. Because God's people had been willing to take the time to seek His face, find out what He wanted, and were ready to bring their loaves and fish to Him, He gave them the privilege of being His co-workers in Berlin. God gives multiple premiums on that which we offer to Him.

Lessons Learned

On the journey to Christ's Lordship, there are huge obstacles placed in our way that need to be demolished before He can work. We have experienced how the concept of achieving faith through prayer often needs to happen before God can move.

The Lordship of Christ extends our prayers through and around obstacles to reach infinitely beyond the barriers that men and the enemy can erect. If we are linked up with the Almighty, He will always find a way to overcome any obstacle placed in His way.

CHAPTER 16

FUNDRAISING IN THE UNITED STATES

"Now to him who can do immeasurably more than all we ask or imagine, according to his power that is at work within us, to him be glory in the church and in Christ Jesus throughout all generations, forever and ever! Amen." Ephesians 3:20-21.

Barriers of Uncertainty

Barriers are not always so tall we cannot climb them. Nor are they solid obstacles we cannot move. They represent varying degrees of resistance to our follow-through. Procrastination is a common symptom. Have you started out on a trip uncertain of the outcome? Have you felt apprehension, yet certainty that whatever the result, it will change your life? The wall of "What if?" is one example. One can also have feelings of inadequacy. Faced with such walls, some people may shy away, not realizing they lose the opportunity to influence the outcome. The key for me was to hold on tightly to what God was doing. I believed He had taken us into partnership in His endeavor, and anything beyond our best was His to manage.

The Flight to Oklahoma City

Around June 1977, Rev. Zanner called and told us that the Division of World Mission had arranged a speaking schedule for me, and I would fly to the USA to raise funds for the new church. The only requirement was that travel costs came from the funds we had already raised. We did not yet have enough cash to buy the ticket and finance the trip. However, in faith, the church board raised the ticket price as an investment in the Lord's plan. They had experienced too much to doubt He would come through this time as well.

Udo Budchinski was a disabled painter, an early retiree because he had worked around too many dangerous paint fumes. He was also a talented amateur filmmaker. The church board asked him to make an 8mm film on West Berlin and the church. At the time, my parents were teaching at European Nazarene Bible College in Büsingen, Germany on sabbatical. My father, Dr. Alvin Kauffman, a graphic artist, volunteered to design a three-color brochure for the trip, which we printed. The Lord blessed this trip in many respects and led in ways I will never forget.

Hugo Danker and I traveled together to Chicago. Our first stop was an Evangelism Conference in Oklahoma City. However, when we arrived at O'Hare, the bulkheads had frozen shut. We missed our connection, and the airline put us up overnight in the Airport Hilton in Chicago. With only half of our luggage in the middle of the night, we finally flagged down a taxi. It did not seem like he knew where he was going. After passing the same intersection for the third time, he finally stopped at a gas station. A few minutes later, we arrived at the hotel. He charged us for all his meanderings. We guessed it was just Chicago.

I had designated this as a faith trip before I left. The Lord was blessing the work. The people were unified, and my spirits were high. These incidents could not make us doubt that God was in this endeavor.

After the Evangelism Conference, the Division of World Mission had scheduled a four-week deputation tour in the Pacific Northwest. Everywhere I went, the people were as excited as we were about what God was doing in West Berlin, and they gave generously.

The Flight to Nampa

One Sunday evening, I was in the home of close friends relaxing and chatting until the phone rang. It was for me. On the other end of the line was the cheerful voice of Janet Stiefel, the

President's secretary at Northwest Nazarene University (NNU). She asked if I would speak in their chapel on Thursday at 10:30 am

That presented a problem. My last service in Washington was on Wednesday evening, a five-hour drive from the nearest airport in Seattle. So, I told her I would love to do it if it were possible to get there on time.

We tried everything. The reservation operator told us that the earliest flight for Boise left Seattle at 6:00 am, stopped several times, and arrived in Boise at 10:15 am when it was on time. Everyone I asked, including the operator, said this flight was never on time. That was not very encouraging. So, I tried Greyhound and Amtrak, hoping they might have an overnight trip. Nothing else was available.

The only hope of arriving even near chapel time was to take the plane, with almost no hope of getting there on time. I called Janet and told her the news. She said that they would have back-up, and I should attempt it. My reply to her was, "If the Lord wants me there, He'll get me there."

I booked the flight. A young man at the church in Kent, Washington, volunteered to drive me to Seattle after the service. The following day was something I was looking forward to. Human planning and manipulation had become impossible. What was God going to do?

Arrival at the airport proceeded without incident. Onboard, my row mate was the vice president of the air controller's union, who had flown this route many times. He asked me about my destination. I told him about the situation and that I needed to be in the chapel by 10:30 am. He chuckled and replied, "I travel this airline and this route often and have never gotten to Boise on time." That was not very reassuring. Still, I answered, "Well, if the Lord wants me there, He'll find a way."

The plane took off five minutes late. My new friend smiled knowingly, but something inside me whispered, "I've got this under control. Don't worry." I took out my Bible to have my devotional time because the early morning hours had not allowed it. The flight route was to take us through Spokane and Coeur d'Alene before landing in Boise. We arrived in Spokane ten minutes late. There was an inordinate delay and scurrying in the plane's entryway. My friend looked at his watch, turned to me, and smiled. I just said, "It's in His hands."

I had just said the words when a service attendant came on board, took the intercom in his hand, and said, "I'm sorry, but there is fog in Coeur d'Alene. We will have to ask those of you flying there to disembark here. The rest of you will fly on to Boise. You will arrive about 40 minutes early."

This time I smiled at my new friend and said, "He knows what He's doing." That incident opened a meaningful conversation on the flight to Boise with that young union executive about the reality of God today. He was moved by what we were experiencing in West Berlin. I wish he had prayed to accept Christ. However, He will never forget that flight to Boise and the crazy man who sat beside him. A few weeks later, the flight controllers went out on strike.

We arrived at the airport 40 minutes early, and Janet was already waiting. I asked her, "Why are you here so early? She replied simply, "I believe in miracles." We spent the drive to the campus praising God for His timing, talking about old times, and arrived 15 minutes before the chapel began. There was enough time to shake the hands of the people who oversaw the chapel and step out onto the stage to challenge 1,500 students to make Christ the absolute Lord of their lives.

I Want to Give It to Help Build the Church

I was visiting my sister in Kansas City and Mary-Esther's older sister and her husband, in Washington, D.C. I was to speak at Capitol Heights the next evening. But a huge snowstorm was already turning into a blizzard. A quick check of the transportation told us that my only hope of getting to Boston before morning, and catching my flights home in three days, was Amtrak. It was the last train to leave out of Central Station. After fighting the worst snowstorm up the coast in half a century, we arrived at Copley

Square at 3:00 am., where I believed I would have a better chance to find a hotel.

I spent two full days and three nights in a Boston hotel, snowed in and looking out my window at the Boston Public Library. The third morning, the Red Line was finally open to Wollaston, the home of my parents. Upon my arrival, Dad whispered that Grammy, my grandmother Kauffman, 89 years old and already legally deaf and blind, wanted me to call her. I gladly did so.

I had worked in my grandfather's printing business from age 12 through college. I had spent most of my summers with them on "The Hill" in the "shop." Grammy and I were extremely close.

That call was characteristic of her. She got right to the point. "Tim, I have an inheritance from my father. As soon as it came, over 50 years ago, I put it in the bank in a savings account and have not touched it since then. It isn't much, but I want to give it to the Lord toward the church's building in West Berlin."

I could not speak. My eyes filled with tears. After all these years, this dear woman, who had given generously to missions and many other worthy causes, had jealously guarded her inheritance. It was probably the only thing in the world that had really been hers. Here, on her deathbed, she gave it to spread the gospel in West Berlin. I was overwhelmed and grateful.

Finally, regaining my composure, I thanked her and told her that I was sure God would reward her for giving Him her inheritance. I could barely hear her voice. She lost her ability to speak in a few days, and two weeks later, she went to be with the Lord. These were the last words she would speak on this side of heaven.

It was a moment I will never forget. I was especially aware of the utterly priceless treasure God had given me in my parents and grandparents.

The trip, embarked upon in faith, had turned out much differently from my initial expectations. We raised funds, but the spiritual uplift and encouragement it brought me were more than I could have imagined. When all the funds were counted, the congregation's contributions, donated labor, and the amount raised, together with a matching-fund gift, was over $400,000. Glory to God!

Two years earlier, we had started out with 2,000 DM for renovations. He did more to supplement our loaves and fish than we could have ever dreamed. He knew we would need much more than the original amount. It was when we raised the money that we realized how much we would really need. *"You give me your loaves and fish, and I will take care of the rest."*

Lessons Learned

Who could have imagined a villa out of my terrible beginning? We continued in His Lordship and went into Stille to ask Him what we should do. The principle He gave us was simple, biblical, and illustrated our situation.

If we are within Christ's Lordship, He expects us to give our all for the task He gives us. But He promises to take care of the rest. It makes no difference how large or overwhelming the job may seem. He will direct and supply all the remaining needs. Living out Christ's Lordship today means allowing Him to break down the walls of our reticence, trust Him, and risk all we have to complete His agenda.

This is a mind-boggling concept. God gives us His all if we stand willing to remove the wall of our inadequacies and allow Him to minister through us with His Holy Spirit.

CHAPTER 17

THOMAS AND ESTHER JOIN US

"And the things you have heard me say in the presence of many witnesses entrust to reliable men who will also be qualified to teach others." (II Timothy 2:2)

Holding on in Faith

Sometimes it is too comfortable in the box, which delimits our ministry. All boxes have four walls. In a tiny but growing church even thinking of beginning a second church can seem to be way out of the box. We had wrestled the concept through with much prayer. Would we be giving away our identity? Can we trust God to grow us in maturity and numbers to be ready? For us, reaching out in faith in that direction formed in my mind when God brought Thomas and Esther to Berlin as interns.

How It All Began

In 1977, as already mentioned, my parents, Dr. Alvin and Alice Kauffman, were on sabbatical, teaching at the European Nazarene Bible College. One student impressed my father with his maturity and scholarship in English, his third language. Thomas Vollenweider had shown such potential that my dad had felt compelled to urge me to invite him and his wife to Berlin for an internship.

Based on that conversation, I asked Rev. Zanner if it would be possible to invite them for a month's practicum (internship). He said that he did not see any problem. Like the other students, they needed eight weeks of training to graduate.

I wrote to them and asked them if they would come. Thomas answered in the affirmative. Finally, we began planning for their arrival in the summer of 1978.

During that time, the struggle with Herr Müller was coming to a head. The church was flourishing despite the persecution. We experienced firsthand how the Church of Christ grows and becomes increasingly dependent on Christ and each other during affliction. They were a delightful couple. We had four delightful and very fruitful weeks with them.

Thomas and Esther Come to Help Start a Second Church

Thomas and Esther returned to the Bible College in Büsingen to finish their last year. They had genuinely impressed us. One day, soon after, in my Stillezeit, I felt impressed to write them a note. So, on the back of an 8" circular smiley on yellow construction paper, I told them how much I had appreciated their stay with us. I mentioned we hoped to start a second church in West Berlin someday. I wrote, "Were we to pick any couple to come as our assistant pastor with this as your primary assignment, you would be our first choice. Would you be interested?"

By then, Thomas had about one more year to earn his B.A. degree in religion. We had a lot of time to let the Lord do His part in the decision process. At that point, everyone understood it to be only a statement of intent.

Just as we were getting to the point of formally asking them to come to West Berlin, Dr. Richard Zanner left to head up the Nazarene work in Africa. Rev. Hugo Danker became District Superintendent. The big question in our minds was whether he would carry through on the project we had negotiated with Dr. Zanner about starting a new church.

Our fears, however, were groundless. Rev. Danker immediately enthusiastically favored Thomas and Esther joining us in West Berlin to plan a new church. The plan was for them to a) serve for a year as our assistant at First Church and become acclimated to the rhythm of the pastorate, b) assist in the coordination and growth of the Home Bible Studies, c) monitor God's work in the various Home Bible Studies, d) establish and lead the *Jungshar* (an activity ministry like Scouting), and e) research and plan for where to begin the second church. We were going to wait on God for where and when.

In July 1980, Thomas and Esther arrived. We all rejoiced and welcomed them into the family. Even though we had looked for an apartment for several months before they came, we had not found one. They were scarce and highly regulated in West Berlin. We put them up in a nearby pension for two months while we finished the one-bedroom apartment in the new church in Grunewald.

Soon after they arrived, we talked about starting a *Jungschar* (pronounced Yoong-shaar) in the fall. Thomas had friends who had successfully integrated new children and their families into their church through this ministry.

Within a short time, almost 20 children between the ages of 9 to 13 were in attendance. They would meet every other week from 3:00-6:00 pm on Saturday afternoons.

The following spring, Hermann Breitenbach, the contractor, came to build the woodwork in the sanctuary ceiling. His pulse increased when he arrived and saw that we had a *Jungschar*. He had formerly been a *Jungschar* leader in another church, and he still loved ministering to children of this age. After finishing the job, he returned to his home church in Gelnhausen and started one. Quickly, many of our congregations in West Germany created one. Not only was the number of *Jungschar* children growing, but also the number of families reached.

Waiting on the Lord and letting Him give the directions had repercussions outside our immediate church circle. Thomas became the first German district *Jungschar* leader and successfully planned and led three *Jungschar* tenting camps. So many children clamored to attend the camps that they had to limit the number attending. They had to organize a camp for youth who had graduated from the program but were still excited about it and wanted to continue participating.

The St. James Church

Soon, however, late in 1981, Thomas needed to lay this effective local and national ministry aside to concentrate on serving their rapidly growing Home Bible Studies in Lichtenrade.

Watching this dedicated young couple grow and blossom along with their soon-to-be congregation was exciting. It was even more gratifying to see the new congregation take on some characteristics of its mother. It had its own personality and its own style of leadership. Both pastors and people were themselves, but it is possible to observe many traits found in the First Church.

I asked Thomas to say in his own words how God had led him and Esther and what the plans were for the *Jakobusgemeinde* (St. James Church of the Nazarene) in West Berlin.

> "Early in my life, the verse in Proverbs 19:21 took on a special meaning for me. *"Many are the plans in a man's heart, but the Lord's purpose prevails."* God knows our future better than we know our yesterday. That is why His Lordship and purpose are all important in my life. He led our paths here to West Berlin, where we have served since 1980. We can think of no place we would rather be than right here where God has placed us."

> "Were we to tell you about all the struggles and victories, the growth spurts, and the difficulties they have brought us, the stories of individuals who had given their lives to Christ for the first time and have become brand new people, we would have to write another volume. At this moment, we find ourselves in an exciting chapter, the pages of which are being written week by week.

> "Because the sanctuary of our Jakobusgemeinde had become too small, we began looking for a piece of land or an adequate building two years ago. Forty real estate agents were searching for us without success. Just a few weeks ago, the Lord saw fit to lay it on a man's heart, marginally connected to the church, to donate a centrally located piece of land to the church as a gift! We erected a new church building on this lot.

"God takes care of His children when they give themselves fully and unconditionally to His Lordship. I do not want to live any other way. Where He leads me in the future, I do not know. That He leads me is my greatest assurance."

Our association with Thomas and Esther is one of our ministry's happiest and most fulfilling experiences.

Lessons Learned

It can be an incredibly positive experience for a young theology student to spend a few months in a full-time internship under an experienced pastor. It is necessary, however, that the pastor involved communicates the excitement and challenge of the pastorate. Just as important are the attitudes and excitement within the church itself. Few experiences have been more satisfying than introducing young pastoral students to the basics of pastoral ministry.

A congregation seeking to practice the Lordship of Christ enables the ministerial candidate to catch this vision and covet such harmony for his or her ministry. The power of Christ's Lordship is contagious. Once we taste it, nothing else can ever satisfy us. We measure everything we experience against it. It is living on the cutting edge of His Kingdom, being out where He is at work, and celebrating His mighty acts. Working through a decision to a consensus taught us that conflict can be good. The trick is to be open to God's words, respect each other, and keep the goal in mind.

CHAPTER 18

THE RENOVATION

"So, we rebuilt the wall... for the people worked with all their heart." (Nehemiah 4:6)

Building the City

Our challenge had always been to accommodate our growing congregation. We had begun attempting to remove the obstacle by planning a modest 800 sq. ft. annex behind the old church. God had said, "no." In our second attempt with a new and larger church, He had again said, "Not yet, I have something better." We were able to exchange our prefab building and property for a villa, only paying for the extra land where the villa was situated. The villa was built in 1898, with over 10,000 sq. ft. of floor space. Not lost on me was that the footprint of the main load-bearing structure was that of a Swiss Cross. It had stood empty for four years. One can imagine the immensity of our task.

We committed ourselves to the cosmetic renovation of the building:

- Dig a four-foot trench around the perimeter of the foundation to insulate the damp basement.
- Paper and paint each of the 15 rooms.
- Scrape and paint twice each of the 50 double wood-framed windows.
- Scrape, clean, and paint each of the 45 radiators twice, and
- Re-landscape the 17,500 sq. ft. grounds, almost a half-acre.

In addition, we contracted out the following needed renovations:

- Fix and rebuild the leaking roof to pre-WWII specifications.
- Install new electrical wiring.

- Remove two load-bearing walls on the first floor to create a 1,500 sq. ft. sanctuary.
- Install a new boiler for the heating system.
- Put in new plumbing and new adequate bathrooms.

After returning from our vacation in August 1980, we began by insulating the outside of the foundation. We dug a trench three feet wide and four feet deep, along with several hundred running feet around the entire perimeter of the building. We dried out, wire brushed the foundation, and then slathered two coats of tar insulation around the building. It took three full Saturdays and four or five people to finish the job.

We then tiled the kitchen and the bathroom for Thomas and Esther's apartment, painted all the windows, papered, and painted the walls and ceilings. Someone donated new kitchen appliances and cupboards from Ikea.

By October 1, when Thomas and Esther moved in, it was yet an unheated one-bedroom apartment with a half-bath. The old boiler was still being replaced. By the time we could get the work done, a month had passed. Poor Thomas and Esther shivered while trying to get those large rooms with 13 ft. ceilings warm with small electric space heaters.

Saturdays were our official workdays. There were 20 people there at one time. They all had to be kept busy. Planning and coordination were necessary. Along with the work, there was a decisive fellowship factor. I overheard people who came for the first time saying, "Had I known there was so much fellowship and fun, I would have come sooner."

Moving In

By the end of February, the construction company had finished removing the two walls, giving us a sanctuary capacity of 150 people. The church board had set the moving-in date for the first Saturday, March 28. Our first service was to be the next day, on Sunday.

THE RENOVATION

But there was a District Assembly, and I was the secretary. We had to drive seven hours through East Germany to get there. I had to be away for five days.

Being the District Secretary, I had to leave all the preparations and drive to Hanau. I put people in charge, told them what needed to be done, and I trusted that all the wallpapering would be finished when I returned.

By the end of Assembly business on Friday, I was feeling restless about the progress in Berlin. I recognized those feelings, and it usually meant that something was wrong. In retrospect, I believe God directed me to return to Berlin early. Finally, I could wait no longer. I arranged for Mary-Esther and John, our son, to return with the others.

I left around 6:00 pm and arrived in Berlin around midnight. After sleeping six hours, I went straight to the church to see how things stood. It is impossible to describe the feelings of tension connected with getting done on time and the necessity of our people working over the weekend.

Arriving at the building site early Monday morning, March 24, I saw a sight I will never forget. I am confident he may still not be aware of how much it meant to me to see him. There stood faithful Thomas Jakob alone on the scaffolding at 7:00 am, wallpapering the last room. I asked him why he was there so early. He was exasperated!

Looking forward to a long weekend off, he came over to find that little had been done. Intent on finishing it, he had been there all night by himself. I climbed up on the scaffolding, and we papered the rest of the room in about two hours.

The rest of the congregation had become weary and had slacked off in their effort. Thomas, too, was tired, discouraged, and dismayed. I explained to him that I had felt led to return early from the Assembly. God had brought me back to stand by his side to let him know his pastor had his back.

Udo, the Painter

Udo, the man who filmed the video for the trip to the United States, stands out in my memory for an additional reason. In his late 40's, he was a gentle, diminutive man who wore coke-bottle glasses because of an industrial accident when he was a painter. Highly acidic paint and fumes had gotten into his eyes and almost blinded him. He had to wear those glasses to see anything at all. One day, early in the renovation process, he came to me and said he would paint all the radiators in the building. I warned him that the 45 radiators needed to be scraped, sanded, and painted twice. He said, "I know; I counted them."

Well, Udo began working on the radiators. He would come in the afternoons for a few hours, sit alone and work on those monotonous monsters until he had one or two of them a few steps farther. Then he would leave as quietly as he came. He worked on them continually and faithfully. First he finished the sanctuary in time, then the other rooms until he had finished all the radiators himself, except that I helped him finish the last few.

God's Protection for Thomas

In renovating, it was necessary to tame the jungle in the front and back yards of the property. Large portions had been left to grow wild during the four years the building had been unoccupied. It was necessary to cut down or transplant giant bushes, cut down several trees and then turn over the soil so we could plant grass and flowers. A 30'x6' concrete slab needed to be broken up and removed from the middle of the backyard. It had served as the floor for the dog kennels.

Then, one afternoon, Thomas was turning over and sieving soil along the driveway from the front gate toward the backyard. He was working quite close to a tree and began hitting roots with the wide edge of a shovel. Suddenly, it hit metal. Not knowing what it was, he hit it again, more vigorously. Because it did not seem to budge, he took a pick and gave it a whack with the pick's point. It glanced off to the side, telling him the piece of metal was round. Then it occurred to him that people still found all kinds of buried World War II munitions in West Berlin. Taking care this time, he dug around the metal object and lifted an ancient but perfectly intact bazooka shell out of the ground.

The firing mechanism had been pointing up. We shudder to think of what might have happened had Thomas made a direct hit with the pick. (We were later told by the police that it was indeed a live shell, and they had detonated it safely.) God had protected him from serious injury.

The Villa Itself

We learned several things about the villa:

- A Jewish Captain in Reichsarmee built it in 1898,
- At first, when the city turned the villa over to us, it could not prove ownership,
- The munitions we uncovered were Russian, and
- It was the police station where I registered my car in 1974.

From this information, we suspect that the Nazi government likely confiscated the building before or during WWII and used it as a command center for police canine control. In the battle for Berlin, the Russians appropriated it because we found hundreds of rounds of Russian munitions, several officers' pistols, several rifles, and much more in the cache. We called the police (it was against the law to possess any firearm or ammunition in West Berlin). They came and took the munitions into custody.

Summary of the Renovation

In the end, the church people donated at least 4,000 labor hours, the equivalent of four people working full-time for six months. They did all the work except the construction, plumbing, heating, and electrical. This was worth at least $100,000 toward the cost of the building's renovation.

Lessons Learned

The authentic heroes of Christ's Kingdom are faithful, even when they do not get any recognition. They are those who submit to Christ's Lordship because they love Him and want to serve Him. It is not the "flash in the pan" that gets the assignment done; rather, the thousands of plodders keep going when the "flashbulbs" have darkened.

The obstacle we constantly battle is the barrier of becoming weary in well-doing. It seems to grow out of the ground even when we oppose it being there. The plodders in Christ's Church have discovered the secret of constantly drawing on His strength to make it through the times where weariness would otherwise immobilize us.

CHAPTER 19

EVEN WHEN THE DREAM IS GONE

> *"If any of you lacks wisdom, he should ask God, who gives generously to all without finding fault, and it will be given to him. But when he asks, he must believe and not doubt."*
> *(James 1:5-6a)*

Giving Up Too Soon

How do you picture the face of Jesus when he said to his disciples, *"O, ye of little faith"*? In my mind's eye, I see a raised eyebrow and a slight smile. What do you think He meant? One thing He might have intended was to say, "You quit too soon. According to my will, you need to hold on until what you have asked actually comes to pass."

There are many reasons for giving up on faith too early.

- We did not genuinely believe God could do it.
- Our faith diminishes as too much time transpires. For example, praying for the salvation of a brother, a son, or a daughter.
- We may have stepped out in faith, but circumstances have made our request impossible. So, we often give up just before God performs a resurrection.

I am sure that there is more Jesus was implying here. However, this wall of doubt can be genuine, particularly when time constraints are looming.

Where Would the Second Church Be Located?

Because of the Home Bible Studies' growth and multiplication in the city's extreme south, we decided that the new congregation would be in Lichtenrade. The municipality of Lichtenrade was near the southern wall separating West Berlin from East Germany. We had been looking for a place for our new church to meet for six months. Thomas and Esther also needed an apartment. An entire house would be the only alternative because the size and zoning laws would limit the use of an apartment.

Thomas had done well in lining up realtors and possibilities. He had narrowed it down to the four houses he wanted me to see. The third house was ideal in every way. It had everything we needed. The only problem was that the owner wanted too much money.

It was already the end of December. Negotiations with the landlord had taken way too long. But we were finally successful in getting him to come down a little. The District Advisory Board had already signed the contract. However, at the last moment, the city informed us that since we were turning our living space into commercial property, it would demand a surcharge equal to the cost of the living space we had rented. The District Advisory Board, paying the rental, reneged on the contract.

On January 10, we informed the church of the decision. The problem was that we were already planning the charter service for the second church on May 21! The mood in the mother church service was one of a let-down, but the Lord helped us through it. After the service, Tomas Rosenhalm approached me. He was the engineer who had come to me three years earlier to start a second Bible Study in Lichtenrade. The board had given its blessing, and that specific Bible Study was a primary reason for our locating the new church there. This usually upbeat and sunny young man was disheartened. It was his baby, too. We stood around in companionable silence. I did not know what to say. "It's all over," he finally lamented. "It took six months to get this far in the negotiations for a house. How can we expect to find anything suitable in six weeks?" The dark clouds of discouragement were etched all over his face. Humanly speaking, he was correct.

I knew he deserved a satisfactory answer because he had been intimately involved in the second church's development from the beginning. His faith had been outstanding. Now, it was being tested to the limit. I am convinced that it is in times like these that the absolute Lordship of Christ is also tested. Our faith either achieves something or remains powerless.

I, too, felt thwarted, but I gathered all the courage I could and said to him: "Tomas, you've been on the church board these last years and have seen how God has come through every time. He will not abandon us now. Do you remember how God gave us this building at the last moment? I know it could not look darker, but I am convinced that by the time the 21st arrives, we will have God's best. If we hold on in faith, I am convinced that somewhere, when we least expect it, God will light a candle in this dark hour that will burn brightly and bring new light on our situation."

I knew I had stepped out a bit bravely, but I was convinced that God was in the new church start, and He would never let Satan's attempts to thwart us succeed. It did, indeed, seem impossible. Here are some reasons:

- We already knew of the limited number of houses on the market, either too expensive or too small. In West Berlin, it takes months to buy or rent a house, even after one finds it.
- No storefronts were available that were suitable or large enough.
- Apartments with living rooms large enough to handle a congregation of 45-50 people are exceedingly rare. Even if we could get one, there would be problems with the neighbors and the city for converting its use.
- In West Berlin, one can almost count the large apartments on one hand, and even when on the market, at least 100 other people are standing in line to get them.
- Whatever we could get would have to be ready for occupancy by May 15.
- We needed not one but two places because Thomas and Esther also needed a place to live.

Any of these factors alone could have prohibited the start of the second church by May 21. Yet, we continued to feel confident that God would provide.

They had already printed the invitations to the charter service without an address. I had sent them around the world. Our prayer now was that the service would not be an open-air meeting.

What a Blessing!

Not knowing about our situation, my parents, along with six students were also in the service. After the service, they invited us to go out to eat. We accepted, but I could not help but continue to reflect upon my conversations after the service, and my first thought was to get my hands on a Sunday Berliner Morgenpost.

Since the housing office did not regulate private real estate classifieds, the Sunday Berliner Morgenpost listed virtually all those classifieds available in the city. I stopped for one at the newsstand on the corner, only to find that there were none. After trying another newsstand with the same success, I remembered the train station in the center of town always had a lot of papers. I live-parked and asked my Dad to wait while I ran in to buy one. They only had two left. I whispered, "Thank you, Lord!" and bought one.

Later that evening, looking for large apartments, I saw an ad for a 1500 sq. ft. apartment in Lichtenrade. Thinking it might be possible, I circled it and gave it to Thomas to check out. On Monday evening, January 11, I called him to see how it went. He exclaimed, "I can't believe it! There is not only one apartment available and unoccupied, but three. It is not in an apartment building but a free-standing house. A company is renovating an old home and the apartments will be ready for occupancy by February 1. We can even pick out our own carpet and wallpaper. The living room on the ground floor is 500 sq. ft., and large enough for a sanctuary. The house is a three-minute walk from the center of Lichtenrade. It is a miracle!"

Barely 24 hours after what had seemed impossible, God had eliminated all our obstacles and lit that candle in our darkness.

On January 28, we signed the lease papers. One of the church's families rented the third floor, meaning we could rent the entire building.

But the work had only begun. Thomas reported that hundreds of square meters of carpet had to be ordered and laid. The whole church prayed that the carpet would come on time for Thomas and Esther to move into their new apartment on Tuesday the 16th, the last potential date for getting ready for the 21st. At 9:00 pm on the 15th, the carpet was still not there. In West Berlin, no firm delivers after 6:00 pm But the congregation kept on praying. At 9:30 pm the doorbell rang. It was the owner of the carpet company himself. He had the carpet in his truck and wanted to put it down. Would that be possible? That dear man worked until 11:00 am and finished one hour before Esther and Thomas arrived with their things. Someone who knows the situation in Berlin told us he had never heard of a firm working all night.

These and several other incidents further prove that God was still in the process of what He had called us to do for His glory. Coming to this point, as a congregation, was something big in the life of our church. We were soon to "give birth" to a second congregation. The church of Christ's Lordship had become reproductive. The joy was profound.

Victory Weekend

Those congregations who actively pursue living in unity under the Lordship of Christ will never be disappointed. The benefits of His Lordship are manifest. May 20-21, 1982, was the culmination of God's demonstration of grace to our congregation. It was a wonderful weekend! Quite a few of our Nazarene family from West Germany celebrated with us.

Saturday Evening, May 20, at 7:00 pm

On Saturday evening, the 20th, at 7:00 pm, we had the send-off for those leaving to start the St. James Church. The service was intermingled with joy and sorrow. An atmosphere of unity was present. The Grunewald Church had given half of its church board, four additional solid members, ten excellent prospects, and all those who attended the Home Bible Studies near the new church. They were the good seed for a fruitful life.

Sunday Morning, May 21, at 11:00 am

On Sunday morning, the 21st, at 10:00 am, we celebrated the dedication of the new Grunewald church building. Over 185 people were in attendance on that cool Sunday morning. Herr Deichert, and other dignitaries from the city, Herr Reinhart Löwe, our architect, Pastor Hugo Danker, the District Superintendent, Thomas, and I were on the platform. Each of the principals said a few words. We sang and prayed, and District Superintendent Hugo Danker preached the celebratory sermon.

Sunday evening, May 28, at 7:00 pm

The charter service for our second church in Berlin, the St. James Church, took place in its newly renovated sanctuary. Around 80 expectant people squeezed into that small sanctuary which could hold 50-55. we raised our joy and gratitude to God for completing all preparations and leading us to this momentous occasion. A new church in West Berlin was born.

Lessons Learned

When we undertake something in Jesus' name, we must consider any seemingly insurmountable walls Satan places in our way to be seen as typical. Such obstacles often arise, attempting to kill the dream just before Christ breaks through to victory. If we had given up, we might never have experienced His triumph.

Christ finishes what He starts. This is true, even when everything points to failure. He does not bring us to the edge of His victory, only to leave us hanging. It was true for the Hebrew children in the wilderness, for Jesus on the cross, and for everything He wants to do through us today. If we know we are under His Lordship, we can know that we can trust Him. In fact, it is by these breakthroughs that we can be confident that He was in it all along. He is worthy of our absolute trust until the very end of life itself.

Looking back, we can appreciate how the power of Christ's Lordship can change people and transform them into effective channels of blessing in His Church. He functions in the life of His body to build unity, but even more important is the way He breaks down the wall of little faith in all of us individually.

CHAPTER 20

TRANSFORMED LIVES ARE HIS REWARD

"Has the community served to make individuals free, strong, and mature or has it made them insecure and dependent? Has it taken them by the hand for a while so that they would learn again to walk by themselves, or has it made them anxious and unsure?" — Dietrich Bonhoeffer, Life Together and Prayerbook of the Bible

When Walls Come Down, Maturity and Usefulness Follow

In the beginning, I stated that working within the total Lordship of Christ, with no barriers, in any group of believers is directly proportional to His complete Lordship in every individual.

Within Christ's Lordship, each person has his or her own story to tell. Every individual has experienced Christ's call to Lordship uniquely. This is because God treats us all as individuals and interacts with us according to our personal needs and personalities.

Throughout this book, we have been concerned with some walls which hinder Christ's absolute Lordship and His power to build His congregation. I have chosen a few people who have embraced Christ's Lordship to tell us how that commitment influenced their lives.

I will introduce each of them and then let them tell you what making Christ absolute Lord has meant for them. Please note that God's interaction with us as individuals should be associated with how Christians interact with each other. Christ's new commandment has charged us to "love one another as I have loved you."

Hans-Joachim Hahn

After we had been in West Berlin for about six months, Hans-Joachim came to West Berlin as a new staff member with Campus. He had just finished his state exams as a sports and English teacher.

We elected him to the church board the following year, and he played a vital role in shaping the spiritual atmosphere of the church. His positive attitude and willingness to let the Holy Spirit work through him was an example to all who knew him.

In 1979, they named him the leader of the blossoming Campus Crusade ministry at West Berlin's two major universities. Later, Hans was called to their headquarters in Gießen, West Germany, where he, in due course, took on the position as director of Campus' Academic Forum for Professors in Germany. God is blessing his ministry.

> "To recognize the Lordship of Christ in the church in Berlin meant for me to see Him concretely in the brothers and sisters He had placed in our midst. It meant believing in them, hoping for them, and loving them as I loved Christ. It meant seeing their personalities through the eyes of faith, seeing, and believing in faith the changes in their lives, which were often still invisible.
>
> "This reminds me of Gertrud Jakumeit. She was old and could not make it to church on her own because her legs were weak. She had suffered much during World War II in East Prussia. During her lifetime, she had fled for her life seven times. She had experienced many disappointments. Finally, she came to our church. She had hardening of the arteries and lived much of the time in memories of the past.
>
> "Because of her destitution on the one hand and that she was a very demanding person on the other, she presented us with some genuine complications. Her apartment was on the way to church for me, so it became my responsibility to pick her up on Sunday morning. Because my ministry was to lead students and businesspeople to Christ and Christian maturity, you can see that Gertrud did not fit into my sphere of influence. God, however, had placed us together in His Church.

"During the many times we drove and talked, I learned to love and respect her as a member of Christ's body. In my time together with her, Christ reformed my thinking and attitudes. For me, this is the power of Christ's Lordship.

"There were disappointments, too. With others, I tried to help a young man give his wish for a wife to Christ. But he determined to take his life into his own hands, left the faith, and experienced overwhelming disappointment. It was difficult for us. Either He is Lord of all, or He is not Lord at all."

Andreas Herling

Andreas had been in Berlin only a few days when he met Hans-Joachim. Having grown up in a Christian home, he considered it essential to find a church home. Since Andreas lived only a few minutes away from the church, Hans suggested he try us out. He came, and we enlisted him right away to play the piano, which he did faithfully and well for six years.

He was part of our church community from his first week as a first-year student until he left Berlin with his Ph.D. in Veterinary Science. His doctoral dissertation revealed a breakthrough in the fight against a particular viral infection in chickens. When he finished his studies, he took a top job as a researcher in one of the world's largest pharmaceutical companies in Frankfurt, Germany. He is now retired.

"People will see our total dependency on God as being weak. In a certain sense, they are right. To live knowing that before God, I am a weak and imperfect individual puts the relationship between the unique God of Scripture in proper perspective and me. Through our capitulation to His absolute Lordship, we have power, stability, and meaning in life through Him.

"The opinions and convictions of most people today, even Christians, are not based on objective facts, but on the spirit of the age in which we live. This spirit is influenced by public opinion, which is itself influenced in substantial part by the mass media. Most people do not realize that their lives and convictions on the world, politics, and even life itself are based on a "trust in 'facts' that we cannot scrutinize.

"The Christian faith is based on historical facts, and the reality of God can be experienced through personal trust in the promises and salvation of God. I am convinced that to be a Christian under the Lordship of Christ is more realistic and better founded than a life without God and its inevitable dependency on the weak foundation of the "spirit of the age."

Annegrit Elsner

Annegrit was a student at the Free University in Berlin. She found Christ through Campus Crusade›s student ministry and attended the church for Sunday morning breakfast a few times. It took several months, but she finally made our church her home. After finishing her studies, she felt God›s call to serve Him in the Campus ministry, and they assigned her to West Berlin. This meant that we would not lose her at first.

In 1983, however, they transferred her to another university and then took on the challenge of training all the new recruits in the Campus student ministry in West Germany. She subsequently married a State Church pastor and transitioned to spreading the sunshine of God's grace in that setting.

"I always wanted to live my life by myself with interference from no one. One of my favorite expressions during my childhood was, "Alone! Want to do it alone!" I could do many things by myself and was successful in everything I tried. But it all had a terrible price - I was alone. I did not care about others, so they did not care about me. This hurt me, of course, but I did not know a way out.

"As a teenager, I entered a friendship with a young man to overcome loneliness, but my drive for independence did not bring harmony. After five years, that relationship failed, as did many others. My life seemed to be a giant puzzle with many pieces that did not fit.

"For the first time in my life, I searched for help. During this search, I attended an evangelistic student's gathering in April 1976. These young Christians impressed me very much. They had a joyous fellowship. They also gave me some answers to my many questions. It was apparent that they accepted me as I was. They stated clearly that their joy even in problems, hope for the future, and peace despite their inadequacy were all because of Jesus living in them. They knew Him personally.

"The same evening, I prayed to invite Christ into my life, and a great peace filled my heart. Reluctantly, I took some steps forward, reading the Bible regularly to find out what God wanted to tell me. I began praying about it, but there was still much fear and apprehension. Could I trust God? Does He really want the absolute best for my life? Does He know best when His commands do not coincide with my ideas and wishes? Step by step, acting out obedience in faith, I learned to trust Him. A fellowship of believers who lived out faithfully helped me very much because their lives showed me the blessings of God. Looking back, I can see the cause of my problems after ten years. I had wanted God to make ME happy, but I had not really submitted to His Lordship.

"In the meantime, He has called me to full-time Christian ministry. Gladly, I share the good news that He wants to be Lord in the hearts of men to show them real purpose in their lives. Jesus Christ has conquered my life with His love, and now I willingly let Him lead me."

The Principle Involved

We have now come full circle. It began with the blessing and direction God gives to children, both natural and spiritual, through the obedience of parents and spiritual mentors. Now we are finishing with church members apprehended and transformed by Christ's Lordship, often through each other. Now, having begun the journey of being formed into Christ's likeness through His Lordship, they have found how to train others to do the same thing in their respective ministries.

> *"You then, my child, be strong in the grace that is in Christ Jesus; and what you have heard from me through many witnesses entrust to faithful people who will be able to teach others as well"* (II Timothy 2:1-2, NRSV).

Lessons Learned

Can anything other than living in unreserved abandon to Christ's Lordship ensure the reproduction of genuine and contagious Christianity in today's world? Many of the walls we encounter on the road to Christ's Lordship, we often erect to protect ourselves from those things we believe will hurt us or rob us of our freedom. As we have seen, He heals us, completes us, and gives us freedom and new horizons we never thought possible.

They are walls erected by the kingdom of darkness that grow to thwart our ministry efforts to advance God's kingdom. These walls should be expected. Jesus called them "The gates of hell." He also said that they would fall against the advance of His Church.

Nothing other than living out total and unreserved abandon to Christ and his Lordship will reproduce genuine and contagious Christianity in our contemporary world. There is joy, struggle, and adventure beyond human imagination awaiting all who will answer God's challenge. He is searching for people over the world for those who will commit themselves entirely to His Lordship, to be His representatives, calling people to be reconciled to the God who loves them.

EPILOGUE

The Call to Frankfurt

The District Superintendent, Hugo Danker, had been talking to me for a while about moving to Frankfurt to assist him by mentoring the younger pastors in the district and pastor a relatively new church on the outskirts of the city. He felt the younger pastors might benefit from someone coming alongside them and their ministry. Mentoring had long brought me great joy.

This point in time seemed to be the culmination of our task in West Berlin. In answer to God's call, we left the walled city. It was one of the most difficult decisions we had ever made. On the one hand, there were many strong personal attachments to the work in West Berlin. On the other hand, there was a real sense that this chapter in our ministry had ended, and it was time to hand over the leadership to capable hands.

We moved to Frankfurt with full confidence in the leadership of Thomas and Esther. In the forty years that have intervened, God's providence has given witness to their God-directed ministry in what is now the capital city of the Bundesrepublik. Originally from Switzerland, this wonderful, talented, resilient, and loyal couple has demonstrated consistently the qualities we saw in them years ago, when we asked them to come alongside us as our associates in the West Berlin ministry.

Thomas and Esther

Even during their internship, and then when they first arrived in 1980, Thomas and I talked a great deal about my hopes for the ministry in the city and my dreams for a compassionate ministry center. Alcoholism, homelessness, and drug addiction were flourishing in the city. It seemed like it would be unreachable, but we prayed and asked God to allow us to serve the needs of those so loved by Jesus.

Based on our conversations during their internship, it became clear that this was an exceptional couple. When we called them to join us in 1980, the Home Bible Studies were already underway. They were asked to oversee the ministry. A working plan was developed out of our collaboration, and the second church was a result. Several Bible Studies outgrew their meeting places and others developed.

When the Wall came down in 1989, it ushered in reunification and opened even more possibilities. In 1992, Just down the street from the St. James Church, on the East German side of the former wall that had come down, an East German Army barracks became available. One thing led to another, and the new government leased the empty barracks to the newly founded Christian non-profit, named *ICHTHYS* (an ancient Christian symbol), to minister to alcoholics, drug addicts, and the homeless. Before they were married, Esther had run a compassionate ministries center in her home near Basel. She became the cook and a mentor/counselor to the kitchen staff for 30 years. Next year *ICHTHYS* will celebrate its 30th anniversary.

The Thrust to the City in Berlin

The year 1993 was declared to be the year of the "Thrust to the City" – to continue the ministry and develop a church planting philosophy and plan its implementation. A pastoral team was formed that continues to meet regularly (once a month). It reflects the special BOND of the Berlin Nazarenes: "We serve the Lord in ONE team and support each other; achievements and victories are shared; we are not in competition with each other!"

The Church Planting Philosophy

Berlin is a city of 3.5 million people, a city with 12 districts with local governments and around 250,000 people in each one.

The vision was that each district should have a church. The main components of this church planting philosophy are:

- The pastors in Berlin work as a team to evangelize the city.
- Churches plant churches.
- Sponsoring the relationship between the mother church and the new church continues for a period of time.
- New churches begin with a nucleus of mature members from the sponsoring church.
- Home Bible study groups in new areas of the city are potential targets.
- Preaching Points serve as extensions and testing grounds for new churches.

Through their leadership, the small groups continued to grow and divide. They soon started a third church, the St. Timothy Church. Later another original Home Bible Studies multiplied and in Steglitz a church was organized. When the Grunewald building was sold a few years later, that congregation joined them. It became the St. John Church. Thomas reflected on his methods while collaborating with me on this Epilogue:

"When reading "Breaking Down Walls", I became completely aware of how much of what has grown and developed under my leadership has developed from the spirit and manner of the founding years. You put a lot into me - by setting an example and guiding what I was later able to realize and pass on myself!"

- The Reichenhallerstrasse (the first property)
- St. James Church, 1982, will celebrate its 40th anniversary next year.
- St. Timothy Church, 1989, closed around 2005.
- *ICHTHYS*, 1992, will celebrate its 30th anniversary next year!
- Prenzlauerberg, 1993 (closed)
- Steglitz, 1995

The direct result of the "Thrust to the Cities," implementing the philosophy of church planting spread out over a six-year period. There were four churches and *ICHTHYS* that began. At the end of the campaign, there were three new churches and the *ICHTHYS* ministry.[1]

The Current Pastoral Team in Berlin and Northern Germany

In 2021, the pastoral team in Berlin and Northern Germany is currently as follows:

- Pastor Martin Wahl, of the St. John Congregation (since 1995) / Director of Northern Germany,
- Pastor Gideon de Jong, of the St. James Congregation (since 2017) / Lecturer at European Nazarene College (EuNC)
- Pastor Johannes Hepp, of the Lydia Congregation (since 2021)
- Pastor Sabine Wielk, of the congregation in Hamburg (since 2016)
- Dr. Wolfgang Köhler, leader/lecturer at our EuNC Extension and part of the Hamburg community
- Katrin Nowak-Dennewill, Director of ICHTHYS, Compassionate Ministry Center
- Thomas Vollenweider and his wife, Esther served the German Nazarene Church for 14 years as the Superintendent and 6 years in North-Eastern Germany. During that time, and up to his retirement, he founded and pastored the Lydia Church, referenced above.

God was incredibly faithful to the little church begun in 1962, by Pastor Gerhard and Sonia Bröhl one year after The Wall was built. There had been many leadership changes and ups and downs in between, but under the capable leadership of Pastor Thorsten Jahnson (1971-1974), it was stabilized. He left us a small but healthy congregation with quality people.

What a blessing to arrive on Easter Sunday of 1974, to our new congregation. The average attendance in June, including the children, was 19 people. They were kind and long-suffering. The love and respect between pastors and people never wavered. Many of them have become friends for life.

They were the faithful people who allowed Christ to become the absolute Lord of their lives. In eight years, the Holy Spirit guided and grew the little church. And then, there was a second church. It is the faithful and blessed ministry of those who came behind us and carried the torch to where it is today. To God be the glory!

Conclusion

As I have already mentioned, soon after we dedicated the St. James Church and the new building in Grunewald, in 1982, the development of the ministry in Berlin was placed in Thomas and Esther's capable hands. Soon thereafter, he was elected District Superintendent and the expansion of the ministry in Berlin began to unfold and develop.

I began this book in September of 2020, with presumably four months to live. God's grace, an anointing service, and the prayers of thousands around the world have brought me to August of 2021. This process of writing, reminiscing, and collaborating with Thomas and Esther concerning the intervening years, has been at the same time humbling and inspiring. Just look at what God has done! All the glory goes to Him!

ICHTHYS

Alongside the growth of the churches, an often less acknowledged but very significant part of the ministry in Berlin is *ICHTHYS*. Next year this bright spot, which Thomas and I dreamed about in the beginning, will celebrate its 30th anniversary.

The Founding of ICHTHYS

When the Berlin Wall came down, the wall of hostility was also breached. The barracks were abandoned that had housed the East German National Army, stationed there to prevent people from escaping into West Berlin. The St. James Church, our second church, under the leadership of Wolfgang and Gisa Schwarzfischer, was located on the southernmost border of West Berlin. One of those abandoned barracks was only a few blocks away from their church. A long-term contract with the government was signed in December 1992, to remodel the facility into a compassionate ministry center. It was organized by members of the St. James Church, and given the name of *ICHTHYS*, an early Christian statement of faith. In contrast to the barracks' original purpose, *ICHTHYS's* mission is to come alongside each client who is seeking liberation from addiction, rescue from homelessness, and deliverance from their old lives.

The renovation of the two buildings was accomplished with financial help from compassionate ministry grants, and the dedicated labor of nine Work and Witness teams from North America.

They began moving into the facilities in January of 1993. When they took possession of the property, they found a poster left on the wall by an East German National soldier in one of the rooms in the barracks, with the following words:

> *"If I rise on the wings of the dawn,*
> *If I settle on the far side of the sea,*
> *Even there your hand will guide me,*
> *Your right hand will hold me fast" (Psalm 139:9-10).*

It seems that the placard was left there by a soldier who was a believer. Considering the changes to come, it could be seen as being prophetic in nature. The center for healing began with 35 residents and 10 full-time workers. Those numbers have held steady over the years of its existence.

Within two years after starting this ministry, 20 decisions were made for Christ, five people were baptized, and a few people joined the church. Clients would participate in group meetings, Christian counseling, and some participated in Bible study groups. Others attend Saint James Church.

Frank Rudersdorf's Testimony

One of the clients who darkened the door of *ICHTHYS* in the early years was Frank Rudersdorf. His rehabilitation, development, and employment have been an incredible story of God's Grace. Here is his story written in his own words in the year 2000.

- "I was broken and had given up. That was my condition when, after my third severe alcohol intoxication within six weeks, I was drunk again and already suffering from severe withdrawal in front of the Christian social worker Ichthys, on December 1st, 1997.
- "Actually, I was already finished with my life, but I wanted to give it one more attempt." "We are afraid for you", this sentence did not let me go. There was someone who worried about me; strangers who made me dare to try this."
- "... After three years I can live again. Today is the best day of my life. During this time, I had the opportunity to complete vocational training, attend a course for addiction help, and above all: I awoke to an interest in new things. My suitcase is now full of stuff for a new happy life."[10]

Katrin Nowak-Dennewill has been the director of this ministry for its entire existence. The reliability of care, financial stability, and constant client census are due to her leadership. From the very beginning, Esther has also been active in the ministry from its very beginning. For many years she served as the full-time cook, mother to the employees, and then part-time, and now even in retirement, she is still volunteering. Thomas has served on the Board since the beginning, and since 2011 has been its chairman, following Rev. Wolfgang Schwarzfischer, who was the founding chairman.

Closing

This ministry of redemption was featured in 1995 in an extensive article in "Church Growth Magazine". Dr. Bill Sullivan, Director of the Department of Church Growth in the Church of the Nazarene, closed the article with these words:

> "Berlin First Church of the Nazarene is exemplary of the New Testament church that took the gospel to the world of its day. It is a model church for today – for the whole world… Compassion and church planting are both top priorities for them.[11]

Now, after almost thirty years, this ministry is as strong as ever. Katrin Novak-Dennewill, her board of directors, and staff has proved again, the power of Christ's Lordship. The product of changed lives, and a holistic approach to evangelism, one that Jesus modeled for us, proves to us that when we allow Him to break down the walls we build to protect ourselves; He breaks down additional walls toward greater impact to the glory of God.

PERSONAL HISTORY

In April of 1986, after four years in Frankfurt, following much prayer, soul-searching, and feeling God's call to teach in the field of missions, we moved to Pasadena, CA, to pursue a Ph.D. in Intercultural Studies at Fuller Theological Seminary. While I was a Ph.D. candidate, I taught Urban Missions, primarily part-time in the Haggard Graduate School of Theology at Azusa Pacific University (APU), and Emmanuel Bible College. During those assignments, there were many opportunities to teach intensive courses in Armenia, Ecuador, Korea, and Guatemala. For the last eight years of ministry, before retirement, we moved across the country in 2000 to become the lead pastor of the Cambridge Church of the Nazarene, a large multi-cultural, multi-congregational church a few steps from Central Square in Cambridge, MA. I was asked to teach as an adjunct professor of practical theology at Gordon-Conwell Seminary, which I did for ten years until 2010.

My retirement years have been dedicated to writing, based on 30 years of pastoring, my degree, and teaching practical theology over a 20-year period. I believe that praxis and theory make each other more effective and relevant.

Writing:

- "*Team, On Three*" 2009 (unpublished). A monograph that describes a flat organizational structure we initiated in 2003 in Cambridge. It describes the need, its implementation, the structure itself, the responsibilities of each leader, a description of its flexibility, and a critique of our initial efforts. It is to date located in the Archive of https://ministryinsociety.org.
- Lessons on the Journey to Christ's Lordship: Walls We Encounter along the Way. (published on Amazon – Kindle Direct Publishing). 2022

- <u>Things I Didn't Learn in Seminary: Short Stories from a Young Pastor in West Berlin</u>. Expresso Publishing,
- Being published in October 2023, <u>Discovering Your Community: The Small Church Finding Its Place in the New Normal</u>." This book employs simple targeted anthropological research. The object is to discover what the local people are expressing, and how the church could meet the needs they discover, both spiritual and life needs.[12]

ACKNOWLEDGMENTS

I am a writer who must write, rewrite, and rewrite again and need lots of help. I want to thank everyone who has helped me on this journey.

- My first thanks go to my wife, Mary Esther. She read every page and the introduction to the book multiple times. She was the only one who could help me with dates, names, and details and give me invaluable insights into the stories. We lived through those years together. This writing has brought some of our earliest years as a team alive again.
- My sister, Mabeth Clem, who for many years edited a weekly periodical, gave me precious guidance in grammar and clarity of thought. Several friends helped me to clarify and articulate what I was attempting to express. Gary Angell and Jim Delp read some of my ideas' initial formulations and gave me wise advice. Bill Gough, a seasoned writer, read it and gave brilliant suggestions for clarity. My friend and mentor, Richard Zanner, wisely suggested adding important context by telling the story of how it all began in the Prologue.
- Thomas Vollenweider, who is still in Berlin, helped me with the dates and events in the years after 1982. Without his help, I could not have written the Epilogue or the story of *Ichthys*, our compassionate ministry center.

ENDNOTES

[1] Dietrich Bonhoeffer, Life Together
[2] Ironically, it was a highway built by Hitler.
[3] Her legs were quite swollen from edema.
[4] The von Bodelschwingh Bethel Institution is a social service community founded in 1867 by Friedrich von Bodelschwingh, Sr., to offer health care and other advantages to the poor, those with inherited defects, and handicapped persons. Nazi influence closed it down, but it had been re-chartered after the war.
[5] We used to call them the "church boss."
[6] It was in Deutsche Marks. I am using U.S. Dollars with an exchange rate of $1.00 = DM 2.25. Remember that it is 1970's money.
[7] The Cold War was still in progress. East and West Germany were still on high alert. West Berlin's final status could have looked much different.
[8] Thomas and I corresponded about the power of mentoring. This is some of what he wrote.
[9] I had registered the church's VW-wagon at that station in 1974.
[10] Rudersdorf, Frank. "Ein Koffer und kaputte Schuhe," WochenSpiegel, Nov. 30, 2000.
[11] Dr. Bill Sullivan, "Grow Magazine," Spring '95.
[12] Because the research is anthropological in nature, you are asking the interviewees their opinion, and gathering information to pray over and consider whether there is a need. Often, when they realize, you are not going to sell them anything, they open up and ask you to help them with a personal issue. This method is open-ended and is useful almost anywhere in the world.

www.ingramcontent.com/pod-product-compliance
Lightning Source LLC
LaVergne TN
LVHW041846070526
838199LV00045BA/1454